Believing
GOD

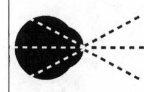

This Large Print Book carries the
Seal of Approval of N.A.V.H.

Believing
GOD

Beth Moore

Walker Large Print • Waterville, Maine

Unless otherwise stated all Scripture citations are from the
NIV, the Holy Bible, New International Version, copyright ©
1973, 1978, 1984 by International Bible Society; other
versions cited are NASB, the New American Standard Bible,
© the Lockman Foundation, 1960, 1962, 1963, 1968, 1971,
1972, 1973, 1975, 1977; used by permission; AMP, the
Amplified Bible, Old Testament copyright © 1962, 1964 by
Zondervan Publishing House, used by permission, and the
New Testament © The Lockman Foundation 1954, 1958,
1987, used by permission; and KJV, the King James Version.

Published in 2006 by arrangement with
Broadman & Holman Publishers.

The text of this Large Print edition is unabridged.
Other aspects of the book may vary from the original edition.

Set in 16 pt. Plantin by Elena Picard.

Printed in the United States on permanent paper.

**The Library of Congress has cataloged the Thorndike
Press® edition as follows:**

Moore, Beth, 1957–
    Believing God / by Beth Moore.
        p. cm. — (Thorndike Press large print inspirational)
    ISBN 0-7862-7663-0 (lg. print : hc : alk. paper)
    ISBN 1-59415-087-7 (lg. print : sc : alk. paper)
    1. Christian life — Baptist authors. 2. Large type books.
I. Title. II. Thorndike Press large print inspirational series.
BV4501.3.M653 2005
    248.4—dc22   2005005320

Dedication

To my beloved church family at Houston's First Baptist Church — I am nearly overcome with emotion as I attempt to find words to express my gratitude and love for you. You have been everything that constitutes a true church "home" to me for more than twenty years. You have loved and supported me and given me a safe place to make mistakes so I could grow. You have been my constant during a time of such change in my ministry life. A place of normalcy and stability, you have been my harbor.

With deepest affection I dedicate this particular book to you because you are a church that has an undeniable history of believing God. We have seen some miracles together, haven't we? Not bad for a bunch of Baptists. God is good . . . and patient.

I wouldn't trade you for the world. Thanks for everything.

With much love,

Beth

As the Founder/CEO of NAVH, the only national health agency solely devoted to those who, although not totally blind, have an eye disease which could lead to serious visual impairment, I am pleased to recognize Thorndike Press★ as one of the leading publishers in the large print field.

Founded in 1954 in San Francisco to prepare large print textbooks for partially seeing children, NAVH became the pioneer and standard setting agency in the preparation of large type.

Today, those publishers who meet our standards carry the prestigious "Seal of Approval" indicating high quality large print. We are delighted that Thorndike Press is one of the publishers whose titles meet these standards. We are also pleased to recognize the significant contribution Thorndike Press is making in this important and growing field.

Lorraine H. Marchi, L.H.D.
Founder/CEO
NAVH

★ Thorndike Press encompasses the following imprints: Thorndike, Wheeler, Walker and Large Print Press.

Table of Contents

Acknowledgments

I have never been more thankful for the people at Broadman & Holman. You have treated me with such kindness. I am humbled by the extra miles you've been willing to go this year on my behalf. I owe you a huge crab cake.

Kim Overcash, how can I thank you enough, especially for working through a meltdown with me over the formatting process? Look at your fabulous work!

I couldn't function without all the true servants and lovers of Christ at Living Proof Ministries. Believing God with you is like the log ride at Six Flags over Texas. The splash of the Spirit makes any down-turn worth it.

Sealy and Curtis Yates, thanks for all your hard work, and for the belly laugh when you finally admitted I'm the weirdest person you work with.

Keith, Amanda, Curt, Melissa, and Danny, you are my wealth. Sunny and Beanie, thanks for keeping me on a leash.

Jesus, Jesus, Jesus. I love you so. You *are* who you say you are.

"You are my witnesses," declares the LORD, "and my servant whom I have chosen, so that you may know and believe me."

Isaiah 43:10

Introduction

Faith is the way believers jump on board with God and participate in countless wonderful things He has a mind to do. Faith happens when believers believe. This book is about developing an action verb faith that invites the exhilaration of holy participation. It's about getting out there where we can feel the wind of God's Spirit blowing in our faces. It's about learning that we don't have to put down the Sword of the Spirit (the Word of God) to raise up the Shield of Faith. The way I see it, that's why God gave us two hands. If we want to live abundantly and victoriously, we must pick up both. To pick up the Sword of the Spirit without the Shield of Faith is to shrivel and dry up in the desert of legalism. To pick up the Shield of Faith without the Sword of the Spirit is to try walking by faith on quicksand.

God thrust the Sword of the Spirit in my feeble hand twenty years ago when He sent me into a young adult Sunday school class as the teacher. Apply that last word loosely. Actually, I was an idiot. I got a brand new Bible for my new journey and I meant to keep it that way. I neglected it. Fumbled it. Dropped it. Opened it. Yawned over it. Whined over it. Cried over it. Begged God to help me with it. Then slowly but surely, one discovery at a time, I fell head over heels in love with it and its brilliant Author. I dug my fingernails into it and vowed never to let it go. I may have a junk-yard of broken vows somewhere but, to the glory of God, that one is not in the heap.

While strengthening my grip on the Sword of the Spirit, God began wedging the Shield of Faith in my other hand so that I'd learn to use them the way He intended: in tandem. Mind you, I thought I had plenty of faith. After all, how much faith does a church-going, church-serving soul need? I would soon learn the answer: a whole lot more than I had. As forcefully as God has ever spoken to my heart, He said, "You believe in Me, Beth. Now I want you to believe Me." The words "believe me" arose out of Isaiah 43:10 like a dead man leaping to his feet. "You are my witnesses," declares the LORD, "and my servant whom I have chosen, so that you may know and believe me."

Believe me. **Believe me**. **BELIEVE ME.** Those two words have echoed unceasingly in my mind ever since. In overriding matters God seems to work in themes with me. I wonder if you've experienced something similar. His themes for me have often come in brief phrases. At this point in my life they consist of three, shed abroad in my heart in this simple *add-on* order:

Love me. Know me. Believe me. *Love Me* seemed to be God's theme for my twenties. *Love Me and Know Me* drove the theme for my thirties. And *Love Me, Know Me, and Believe Me* became His mouthful for my forties.

For reasons known only to a forgiving God, I've spilled quarts of ink through Bible studies and books in attempts to share a passion to love God and know Him. I will continue to express these holy obsessions in one way or another as long as God wills. The book you now hold in your hand is my attempt to articulate my own personal journey toward obedience regarding the third command: *Believing God.* Not here and there in crises but as a lifestyle. The piercing voice of the prophet Isaiah proclaimed its importance: "If you do not stand firm in your faith, you will not stand at all" (Isa. 7:9).

The last seven years have been terribly difficult in countless ways but learning to practice action verb faith in the midst of them has been the most exhilarating adventure I've ever had. In words truer to my sanguine nature, it's been a blast. Not the trials, mind you, but the invitation to believe God for victory — and even favor — in the middle of them. Yes, I've seen miracles. Some of them were huge. But God's daily interventions have awed me the most and left me shaking my head in amazement that the God of the universe would be so attentive to my trivial challenges. I have never before so richly experienced the revelation of John 1:16: "From the fullness of his grace we have all received one blessing after another."

My prayer is that God will do the same for you. I am convinced that Christ is always the initiator of matters concerning faith (Heb. 12:2). So if I'm on target, you've neither stumbled onto this book nor accidentally found it in your hands. Christ is initiating a fresh anointing of faith in your life, Dear One. Wise you are if you want to "test the spirit" (1 John 4:1) and proceed with caution on subject matter like this. I am as reluctant to pick up books on faith as anyone could possibly be. We live in a religious culture where faith practices have been distorted and twisted to serve man rather than God. Our dilemma is whether or not we will allow the misuse and abuse of the topic to keep us from appropriate practices of faith. After all, without faith it is impossible to please God (Heb. 11:6). Keep in mind that most heresy is truth twisted. Let's get into the Word together and see if it can be unraveled and powerfully put into practice.

"This is to my Father's glory, that you bear much fruit, showing yourselves to be my disciples."

John 15:8

Chapter One

Your Promised Land

Is it working? Your belief system, that is. Is it really working? God's intention all along has been for the believer's life to work. From divine perspective toward terrestrial turf, God meant for His children to succeed. God stated unapologetically in Joshua 1:8 that conditions exist under which "then you will make your way prosperous, and then you will have success" (NASB). Are our Christian lives successful? Are they achieving and experiencing what Scripture said they would? In a recent sermon my son-in-law preached, Curt told us the only way we were going to impact the world and the next generation is to prove that our faith in Christ is real and that it works. For countless Christians I'm convinced it's real. My concern is whether or not we have the fruit to suggest it works.

I fear the reality of most Christians differs dramatically from our theology. We bear little resemblance to a church causing the gates of hell to tremble. I squirm as I suggest that the gap between our theology and our reality is so wide we've set ourselves up for ridicule. The sad part of it is that some of us are working pretty hard at something that is hardly working. Why do we spend so much time and energy on spiritual exercises with few effects while the rest of the world sleeps in on Sundays? Why are some of us getting up before dawn to have a quiet time with effects drained to the dregs by noon? Why are we running out of ink in our highlighters marking Scriptures that rarely jump off the page and onto our pavement? Why are we doing everything we can to convince others to do something that hasn't worked terrifically well for us? Why won't some of us admit that for all practical purposes the present belief system of most Christians isn't working?

Certainly those of us who have accepted Christ as our Savior have received the automatic and glorious result of eternal salvation. However, the primary reason God left us on earth after our salvation was for our Christianity to "succeed" right here on this turf. We're getting by but getting by, was never our destiny. We were meant to be profoundly effective. Why have we accepted average? Are the few effects most of us see and experience all Christianity has to offer? Is this it? All we can expect? If so, someone out there needs to feel sorry for us.

I'd volunteer except that I no longer buy it. Our status-quo system of contemporary Christianity isn't working, and I'm bucking it. Thankfully, so are a number of others. Some of us no longer want to play like the emperor has new clothes when he's walking around, as my grandmother would say, as naked as a jaybird. The church, comprised of all believers in Jesus Christ, is generally pretending she's cloaked with kingdom power and effectiveness while in reality she has exposed herself in power-lessness to the ridicule of the world. We can't blame the devil. For the most part we've dumbed-down New Testament Christianity and accepted our reality as theology rather than biblical theology as our reality. We've reversed the standard, walking by sight and not by faith. We want to be the best of what we see, but frankly what we see is far removed from God's best.

A few months ago I was taking my usual route on my morning walk when I came upon a simple scene with telling application. Four ducks were splashing in a mud puddle in the sidewalk while a large, pristine pond was just over a small hill. I stopped in my tracks and stared. I felt like God was saying to me, "Beth, that's my church. My blood-bought, Spirit-promised church splashing in a mud puddle with a sea of living waters within her reach. Just on the other side."

Trust me. No one has been covered with more mud from puddles-settled-for than I. Forgive me if my zeal is too easily interpreted as condemnation or criticism. What a hypocrite I'd be! If a mistake can be made, I suppose I've made it. In fact, my past record of failure, defeat, and pitiful mediocrity is exactly why I'm heaven-bent on sharing this message with you. If God can empower me to move from the mud puddle to the pond with such broken wings, wobbling legs, and webbed feet, I can assure you He can move you.

Beloved, God has made us promises. Real ones. Numerous ones. Promises of things like all-surpassing power, productivity, peace, and joy while still occupying these jars of clay. Few of us will argue the theory, but why aren't more of us living the reality? Like the children of Israel, I believe many of us are wandering in the wilderness with the Promised Land just on the other side of the river. This book has one primary goal: to encourage any Christian who will listen to move to his or her personalized place of divine promise and to flourish.

Blessing is bowing down to
receive the expressions of divine favor
that in the inner recesses
of the human heart and mind
make life worth the bother.

God not only approves of New Testament believers applying the concept of a Promised Land, He insists on it in the third and fourth chapters of the book of Hebrews. Our Promised Land and Sabbath rest culminate in heaven, but I'd like to suggest that an earthly Promised Land exists for you and an earthly Promised Land exists for me. How might we define our land of promise? Your Promised Land is the place where God's personalized promises over your life become a living reality rather than a theological theory.

Need a few examples? The parallels and subsequent applications we can draw from the children of Israel and their land of promise are numerous, but just for starters . . .

1. *God promised us a place of blessing.* God's willingness and unwavering desire to bless His people is one of the most repetitive concepts in both testaments of His Word. He is the Giver of all good gifts and greatly exults when a child cooperates enough to receive some. New Testament believers were promised blessing for obedience as surely as the children of God in the Old Testament. The Promised Land was a place of promised blessing to those who followed the precepts of God. When you and I find our places in Christ where God can freely fulfill His promises to us, we will also experience immeasurable blessing. Blessing is defined by neither ease nor worldly possessions nor stock-market successes. Blessing is bowing down to receive the expressions of divine favor that in the inner recesses of the human heart and mind make life worth the bother.

2. *God promised us a place we could live.* God didn't promise the children of Israel a place they could visit. He promised them a place they could settle and dwell in blessing. A land they could possess. A place they could find Sabbath rest. According to John 15, New Testament be-

lievers have likewise been called to a place of abiding. Living. Dwelling. I finally came to a point in my Christian walk where I grew bone weary of inconsistency being my only constant. Occasional wisps of authentic spiritual living only multiplied my frustrations. I then knew a place of fullness and effectiveness in Christ existed, but at best I was a drop-in. My soul needed a place it could live. I longed for my defeats to be infrequent visitations, not my victories. Beloved, our personalized lands of earthly promise are places we're invited by God to dwell in Christ. It's high time we stopped dropping in and started taking up residency.

3. *God promised us a place where He brings forth a great harvest.* As much as any characteristic of the Promised Land, God promised that it would be fruitful. Many of us have heard it characterized as a land of "milk and honey," but additional Scriptures are far more descriptive. For instance, Deuteronomy 8:7–9 says: "For the LORD your God is bringing you into a good land — a land with streams and pools of water, with springs flowing in the valleys and hills; a land with wheat and barley, vines and fig trees, pomegranates, olive oil and honey; a land where bread will not be

scarce and you will lack nothing; a land where the rocks are iron and you can dig copper out of the hills."

John 15 again supplies us with a New Testament Promised Land parallel for every follower of Jesus Christ. The eighth verse says, "This is to my Father's glory, that you bear much fruit, showing yourselves to be my disciples." Not some fruit. Much fruit. Beloved, can you accept the truth that your heavenly Father wants to show His glory through using your life to bear tremendous fruit? Your personalized Promised Land is the abiding place where you get to see God keep the promise of a great harvest through your life.

God has far more in mind than bringing forth one kind of fruit from your life. The harvest God desires to produce has the potential of abounding variety. I believe the promises God made to the Israelites for their Promised Land in the tangible realm parallel ours in the spiritual realm. You and I weren't called to become machines of mass-but-monotonous production. Just when we decide our lives are all about figs, God starts mixing up the soil underneath our feet to bring forth some pomegranates. Have you too quickly decided that what you have done or what you are doing is all you'll ever do? Ah, God's far too creative for that. May God use our present journey to shake up some soil.

Perhaps my favorite part of Deuteronomy 8:7–9 is that the Promised Land was an abiding place where God's people would lack nothing. Need a New Testament parallel? Second Peter 1:3–4 tells us that "his divine power has given us everything we need for life and godliness through our knowledge of him who called us by his own glory and goodness. Through these he has given us his very great and precious promises, so that through them you may participate in the divine nature and escape the corruption in the world caused by evil desires." Our personal Promised Lands are the places we accept those "very great and precious promises" and appropriate "everything we need for life."

If you can't imagine God ever delivering you from the corruption of evil desires and bringing forth a great harvest through your life, you've bought into the lie that God's promises don't apply to you. The Amplified version of Ephesians 2:10 says that you and I are "God's [own] handiwork (His workmanship), recreated in Christ Jesus, [born anew] that we may do those good works which God predestined (planned beforehand) for us [taking paths which He prepared ahead of time], that we should walk in them living the good life which He prearranged and made ready for us to live."

God knew you before you were formed in your mother's womb and planned good works for you that would bring forth much fruit. According to Acts 17:26, God even determined the times and places set for us to live on planet Earth most conducive to our personalized harvests. Too much predestination for you? Here's the catch: we don't have to cooperate. We can live our entire lives as Christians and never fulfill the glorious plan God tailored for us in advance.

Ephesians 1:18 says, "I pray also that the eyes of your heart may be enlightened in order that you may know the hope to which he has called you, the riches of his glorious inheritance in the saints." Our glorious inheritance in Christ is not meant for heaven alone. The primary context of Ephesians 1 is the impact of our heavenly inheritance on our earthly existence. God knows the plans He has for us, Dear One, but He will not force them on us. Don't miss the word *hope*. Nothing about your calling or mine is compulsory. God is going to accomplish His agenda regarding heaven and earth no matter what you and I do, but we get to decide whether we're going to be part of His process in our generation. Our callings remain a hope until we allow the eyes of our hearts to be enlightened and choose to accept them.

4. *God promised us an abiding place of great victory over our enemy.* From the moment God first issued the promise of land to Abram, He described its occupants as quickly as its perimeters: "To your descendants I give this land, from the river of Egypt to the great river, the Euphrates — the land of the Kenites, Kenizzites, Kadmonites, Hittites, Perizzites, Rephaites, Amorites, Canaanites, Girgashites and Jebusites" (Gen. 15:18–21). Our Promised Lands are characterized by the presence of victory, not the absence of opposition.

Promised Land theology becomes an earthbound reality only to those who cash in their fear and complacency for the one ticket out of their long-inhabited wilderness.

Earlier I asked you if your present belief system was working. One way we can measure our belief system's effectiveness is to examine how consistently our biblical position as "more than conquerors" (Rom. 8:37) is fleshed out in our reality. The children of Israel showed they were God's conquerors on earth by conquering. Victory always assumes a counterpart defeat. We will never take our places as "more than overcomers" with nothing to overcome. We will never be victors without opponents. As we will continue to see in our journey, God gave the Israelites the Promised Land but told them they'd have to take what was theirs in fierce battle. Why? Probably one reason was so they'd develop the strength to keep it once they conquered it. Surely another was to let them experience the thrill of victory that only a battle hard fought can bring. In God's economy, much of what is worth having is proved worth fighting for.

Like the Israelites, you and I have been promised spiritual ground for great and abiding victory on a turf where our enemy stands in defiance. If you're not presently occupying your Promised Land, rest assured the devil is. Are you going to stand by and let him get away with that? God has given you land, Beloved, but He's calling you to go forth and take it. Your enemy is standing on your God-given ground daring you to take possession of it. Are you going to let him have it? Or are you going to claim your inheritance? Possession is the law of the Promised Land. Red Rover, go over.

The Creator of heaven and earth — the One with the entire universe and its riches at His disposal — knows you by name, has planned a Promised Land for you, and longs to bless you. He wisely reserves the right to require your cooperation. Many promises of God are unconditional, but His promises of full-throttle blessing, abiding, fruit-bearing, and conquering are not. Nothing in your life or mine is worth forfeiting the places of promise where our own 1 Corinthian 2:9's are fulfilled. What God has prepared for you is more than your ears have heard, your eyes have seen, and your mind has ever conceived. Promised Land theology becomes an earthbound reality only to those who cash in their fear and complacency for the one ticket out of their long-inhabited wilderness.

". . . His incomparably great power for us who believe."

Ephesians 1:19

Chapter Two

One Ticket
Out of the Wilderness

Several years ago I left a doctor's office with a handful of prescriptions so complicated to take that I threw them in the trash on my way out of the building. I decided being sick was less trouble. I'm a simple-minded woman, and I like uncomplicated answers. Needless to say, human life is fearfully and wonderfully complex, making intricate and procedural solutions often necessary. I'm happy to report, however, that the overriding questions raised in chapter 1 don't have complicated answers.

Why isn't our present practice of Christianity working, and why don't we see more of God's promises fulfilled? The same reason the practices of the Israelites in the wilderness didn't work and they never reached the land they'd been promised. Like them, we can be dramatically delivered from bondage, leave our Egypts, and yet never make it to our Promised Lands. We, too, can find ourselves lodged in a desolate wilderness between. Hebrews 3:19 supplies the one-word explanation: "So we see that they were not able to enter, because of their unbelief."

Unbelief. Oh, they believed in God. Their oversight was that they simply didn't believe the God they believed in. They talked a good talk, but their walk did nothing but tread sandal tracks in desert circles. The Israelites of the Exodus were promised land, blessing, productivity, and victory; but the masses never saw their theology become a reality. The question raised in the wilderness wanderings was not whether the Israelites belonged to God or where they would spend eternity. The place the chosen people of God would spend their earthly existence was the question. The King James Version of Hebrews 3:17 underscores the outcome most vividly: their "carcasses fell in the wilderness."

You and I can be safely tucked in the family of God and have the full assurance of a heavenly inheritance without ever occupying the land of God's fulfilled promises on earth. We can completely miss our earthly destinies, and our carcasses, too, can fall in the wilderness. While Keith and I were in Africa last summer, we came upon the spine-tingling sight of a cow's entire carcass polished to the bone by a lion. God's Word tells us Satan is like a roaring lion seeking whom he may devour (1 Pet. 5:8). Perhaps, like me, you could say that Satan has tried one ploy after another to destroy your life, your witness, and your fruitfulness. Will we let him have the satisfaction of cleaning our carcasses to the bone because we let them drop in a desert of defeat? God forbid.

I don't want to be counted among the faithless who never claimed the land God promised them. All that will matter about our earthly lives when we receive our heavenly inheritance is whether we fulfilled our callings and allowed God to fulfill His promises. I know I'm going to make it to heaven because I've trusted Christ as my Savior, but I want to make it to my Canaan on the way. I want to finish my race in the Promised Land, not in the wilderness. You too? Then we have to cash in our fear and complacency and spend all we have on the only ticket out: BELIEF.

> Faith is the only thing that will ever close the gap between our theology and our reality.

Lots of it. The reason most of our present belief systems aren't working is because they are big on systems and small on belief. What you and I need is a fresh belief in our systems. That's what this book is all about. Faith is the only thing that will ever close the gap between our theology and our reality. Throughout these pages we're going to explore the huge premium God places on living, breathing faith.

We'd be hard pressed to find a more consistent priority God places before His people in either testament. I believe Scripture will reveal to us through our journey that nothing is more important to God than our faith. Yes, love is His greatest commandment, but any of us who have accepted the mammoth challenge of biblical love in difficult circumstances can testify how much faith was required for obedience.

God is not the only one prioritizing the issue of our faith. Satan also has no greater focus in a single one of our lives. Though he is no match for God, he is a powerful and dangerous foe of believing man. Not coincidentally, both God and the devil are targeting our faith because the stakes are so high. We'll look at two vital issues at stake presently, then consider a number of others in the chapters ahead.

"Thou has created all things, and for thy pleasure they are and were created." — Revelation 4:11

---

1. *First and foremost, "without faith it is impossible to please God"* (Heb. 11:6). That's one reason we may as well accept faith challenges as a fact of life and not be shocked or feel picked on when they come. God brings them to build our faith, prove us genuine, and afford Himself endless excuses to reward us. He delights in nothing more than our choice to believe Him over what we see and feel. Revelation 4:11 (KJV) adds another important dimension to God's pleasure in our exercise of faith: "Thou has created all things, and for thy pleasure they are and were created." Viewing these two Scriptures side by side, we infer that our ultimate purpose for existence is to please God; therefore, if we don't exercise faith, we will never fulfill our reason for being.

If you haven't yet developed a trust relationship with God, the concept of living your entire life to please Him may unnerve or even offend you. I understand. I, too, have battled tremendous trust issues in every relational dimension. I have not always found man trustworthy (not man, me), but God has never failed to live up to His Word in our relationship. I believe you will find Him completely trustworthy too. God is for us, Dear One. Even His commands are for our safety, liberty, and blessing (Deut. 10:13). Yes, God calls us to surrender our own agendas on the altar of His will, but Romans 12:2 reminds us that God's will for us is good, pleasing, and perfectly suited. When all is said and done, the biggest sacrifices of our lives will be when we chose our own way and forfeited God's pleasing will for us.

The last thing Satan wants is for God to be pleased. Remember, Satan's ultimate gripe is with God. Our enemy's chief goal is to get back at God for not putting up with his arrogance and his desire to be "like the Most High" (Isa. 14:14). Satan cannot touch God, so he does everything he can to get to His heart by getting to His children. "For whoever touches you touches the apple of his eye" (Zech. 2:8).

The pleasure of God is not the only premium at stake in our exercise of faith. Both God and Satan know that . . .

2. *Faith works.* If you're not already convinced, I'm counting on God to prove the principle to you over the pages to come. In fact, nothing works like faith. Its God-ordained dividends are astronomical. Unfortunately, so are the costs of its absence. Biblically speaking, faith is without equal in its effects upon the human life precisely because God is without equal and faith is the normative invitation He answers with proof. Christ can operate any way He desires, but His usual mode of operation regarding His followers is "according to your faith will it be done to you" (Matt. 9:29, among many other similar references). Whether or not we like the concept, Christ loves to respond to us according to our faith. I used to bristle over the idea, too, until I started exercising a little more belief and experienced completely unexpected and exceeding results. I've noted a pretty reliable ratio along the way: The less faith we have, the more we tend to resent the concept. If you're bristling right now, stick around. I have a feeling you'll like the concept better at the end of this book.

If faith works, we want to make sure we

know what faith is. This is the perfect time to nail down exactly what this book means when we talk about "believing God." In New Testament Greek, the word *pistis* means "assurance, belief, believe, faith, fidelity."[1] The Hebrew meaning is similar in nature and practice. In our series we will use various tenses of the word *belief* interchangeably with the word *faith*. With few exceptions the words *faith, belief, believing,* or *believe* are all translated from some form of the word *pistis* in the New Testament. (One exception is in Hebrews 10:23 where *faith* is translated from the word *elpis* which can be translated as *expectation, confidence, faith,* or *hope*. Even the rare exceptions have similar meanings.) When I use the phrase *believing God,* therefore, you can think of it interchangeably with having faith in God. I prefer the former expression for our purposes because it has far stronger implication of action. We're going to discover that faith is not just something you have. It's something you do. The kind of faith you and I are going to study can turn a noun into an action verb quicker than you can say, "See Spot run."

Nothing on earth compares to the
strength God is willing to interject into
lives caught in the act of believing.

Picture the page from an old first-grade
primer. Spot wasn't about to run. Nor was
he in a past-tense heap of exhaustion by
his water bowl. "See Spot run" inferred he
could presently be caught in the act of running. What does seeing Spot run have to
do with believing God? Verb tenses! As
strange as this may seem, the entire prem-
ise of this book sprang to life like a runner
off his mark through a New Testament
verb tense. I'll illustrate through a comparison of Scripture taken from the same
chapter. (The emphasis in both segments
is mine.)

"And you also were included in Christ
when you heard the word of truth, the
gospel of your salvation. Having
believed, you were marked in him with
a seal, the promised Holy Spirit."
— Ephesians 1:13

Ephesians 1:13 says, "And you also were
included in Christ when you heard the
word of truth, the gospel of your salvation.

Having believed, you were marked in him with a seal, the promised Holy Spirit."

Ephesians 1:18–20 says, "I pray also that the eyes of your heart may be enlightened in order that you may know the hope to which he has called you, the riches of his glorious inheritance in the saints, and his incomparably great power for us who *believe.* That power is like the working of his mighty strength which he exerted in Christ when he raised him from the dead."

The New International Version (NIV) uses two important and distinctive verb tenses of the same basic word *believe* in verses 13 and 19. Verse 13 speaks of Christians "having believed." This faith action refers to the exercise of belief that leads to salvation. Each of us who are Christians heard the gospel message at some point and from then on chose to believe it and receive it. Because we exercised this faith action, we immediately became Christ's. We were given His Holy Spirit and marked with a seal. This faith action was exercised in the past with obviously radical results.

The Greek verb tense of the word *believe* in the second segment I listed for you (Eph. 1:19) is the most vital to our series. It is called a present active participle. I'll explain the tense to you as one of my

Greek instructors explained it to me: "Beth, when you see a present active participle Greek verb, you can think of the word *continually* preceding the verb." In other words, the promise given in verses 19–20 is not applied to those "having believed" in verse 13. Rather, it is applied to those who are presently, actively, and, yes, continually *believing God.*

My point? Our glorious walk with God began with an act of faith that brought us into relationship with Jesus Christ as our Savior, but it doesn't end there. *Having believed* in Christ, we've been called to *continue believing* all He came to do and say! Tragically, some *having believed* in Christ have believed little *of* Christ since. He who began a work in us has far more He wants to accomplish. God is calling you and me to leave the life of passivity bred by a past-tense view of faith and get caught in the act of present-active-participle believing. Nothing in life could be more exciting and exhilarating. Let me just go ahead and say what this certified sanguine is thinking: Nothing on earth is more fun than faith. If you decide to sign up for the great adventure of faith, I can promise you'll never get bored.

A Christian practicing present-active-participle belief in God is Satan's worst nightmare. One reason is clearly stated in Ephesians 1:18–20 on page 40. Read it again and absorb just how effectively faith works according to the last statement I quoted from the segment. Let this truth be written in permanent marker on the wallpaper of your mind: God exerts an *incomparable* power in the lives of those who continue believing Him. Hear it again: Nothing on earth compares to the strength God is willing to interject into lives caught in the act of believing. Under the inspiration of the Holy Spirit, Paul likens it to the stunning power God exerted when He raised His Son from the dead! Do you hear that, Beloved? Can you think of any need you might have that would require more strength than God exercised to raise the dead? Me either. God can raise marriages from the dead, and He can restore life and purpose to those who have given up. He can forgive and purify the vilest sinner. God's specialty is raising dead things to life and making impossible things possible. You don't have the need that exceeds His power. Faith is God's favorite invitation to R.S.V.P. with proof.

The pleasure of God and a power beyond compare: just a few things at stake in matters of faith.

"... Take up the shield of faith, with which you can extinguish all the flaming arrows of the veil one."

Ephesians 6:16

"You will have these tassels to look at and so you will remember ..."

Numbers 15:39

Chapter Three

Preparing for Wars and Wonders

Just like the children of Israel, we will always have an enemy that wants to keep us out of our Promised Lands. In our previous chapter we discussed a few reasons why. Nothing does more damage to the power of darkness in this world system than a present-active-participle believer. If we're going to win our battles, however, we're going to have to wise up to some of Satan's schemes and prepare in advance for victory. Our warfare is complicated by opposition that is much harder to identify than human Hittites, Perrizites, and Amorites. In Ephesians 6:12–13, the apostle Paul tells us that "our struggle is not against flesh and blood, but against the rulers, against the authorities, against the powers of this dark world and against the spiritual forces of evil in the heavenly realms. Therefore put on the full armor of God."

Among the strategically prescribed pieces of armor, the King James Version (KJV) tells us, "Above all, taking the shield of faith, wherewith ye shall be able to quench all the fiery darts of the wicked" (v. 16). Why "above all" do we need to learn to use our shield of faith? Because the shield is the armor's armor. The ancient warrior hoped the fiery dart never reached the helmet or the breastplate. A direct hit on any of the other defensive covers could still stun and bruise even if it didn't wound. The warrior's goal was to extinguish any oncoming dart with his shield in order to diffuse all potential damage. When the warrior's shield was down, the other pieces of armor were vastly more vulnerable.

The same is true in our warfare. Our toughest battles will invariably concern matters of faith — times when we're tempted to think God's Word and His ways won't work for us, that He has abandoned us, let us down, or failed to come through for us. If Satan can get us to drop our shield of faith, he knows we can't remain standing for very long. Firsts have great importance in Scripture. Do you know the first recorded words that ever came from the serpent's mouth?

"Did God really say . . . ?" (Gen. 3:1).

He used the spade of deceit to sow doubt. Satan, posing as the serpent, couldn't keep Eve from believing in God, so he did the next best thing. He baited her, tempting Eve not to believe God or trust His motives. Her walk was crippled, her doubt was contagious, and the couple lost the land God had placed under their feet. You see, when Eve dropped her shield of faith, every other piece of spiritual armor became vulnerable. Satan knew she wouldn't remain standing for long. When she fell, she fell hard. I know the feeling.

"Above all," you and I need to learn to take up our shield of faith. We also desperately need to know the Word of God and wield the Sword of the Spirit so that when the enemy slyly suggests "Did God really say . . . ?", we can know the answer emphatically. When we respond to attacks of doubt, distortion, and deceit with the truth of God's Word, the fiery dart is extinguished and the enemy takes another hit. I owe him a few. You too? Then let's commit to take this present faith challenge seriously.

> Our toughest battles will invariably concern matters of faith — times when we're tempted to think God's Word and His ways won't work for us, that He has abandoned us, let us down, or failed to come through for us.

I am praying with all my heart that this won't be just another book. I love to read, and my hands are invariably velcroed to one Christian book or another. All have encouraged me, and some have been life changing. Believing God isn't a book, however. It's not a Bible study either. It's a lifestyle. I'm praying with all my might that the faith adventure suggested in these chapters has only begun when you read the last page. Beloved, I want huge things to happen in your life because you have a huge God. Because I want so desperately for you to surrender your life to action-verb faith, I have asked God for something big on your behalf. Through the power of Jesus' name, I have asked Him to show you a wonder or somehow visibly bless your diligent cooperation early in the process so that you will be encouraged to press on. My request of God is certainly not just for results but because nothing is like experiencing the affirming, undeniable nod of God. I'm praying with all my might that He will do something obvious to show you you're on the right track so that when seasons come with less evidences, you'll have the unwavering assurance that God is believable.

When we respond to attacks of doubt, distortion, and deceit with the truth of God's Word, the fiery dart is extinguished and the enemy takes another hit.

I'm also requesting something of you. I'm asking you to consider making a commitment to three specific faith practices I'll share with you through the remainder of this chapter. Together they enhance an environment in and around you that invites the pleasure and power of God. I am by no means suggesting we play Let's Make a Deal with God or try manipulating Him for miracles. God is not a paid performer and would not be shy to show His disapproval over an inappropriate approach. Let's be careful, however, that we don't err in the opposite extreme of faithless caution. Keep this concept ever before you in the chapters to come:

A big difference exists between trying to manipulate God and to give us what we want and cooperating with God so He can give us what He wants. The latter is our goal.

Once you familiarize yourself with the three faith actions, you'll need a time frame in which to practice them. After you finish the chapter, if you're willing, please spend some time in prayer and ask God how long He'd like you to make these commitments. Most of us need much longer than a few days to form new habits, so please consider a longer time frame. Forty days can be an effective length of time. In the *Believing God* Bible study curriculum, we make our commitment for nine full weeks. Three months is another effective time period for developing a new approach to life. Pray about it and stick with it for the season God and you set. If you forget or blow the faith practices one day, get back to them the next.

The exercises I will share with you are immensely motivating to me. They are ways God has given me to demonstrate externally a work He is accomplishing internally. I pray they will exhort you as well.

The three faith practices follow:

1. *Practice raising your shield of faith.* The well-equipped ancient warrior we talked about earlier didn't wait until he was facing the fiercest battle of his life to learn how to use his shield. He practiced in advance. God taught me a specific way to practice taking up my shield of faith, and I use the method constantly in and out of heated battles. He equipped me with a five-statement pledge of faith that encompasses virtually everything we're challenged to believe. Together they form the spine of this book:

> **God is who He says He is.**
> **God can do what He says He can do.**
> **I am who God says I am.**
> **I can do all things through Christ.**
> **God's Word is alive and active in me.**

Though I often say these five statements silently to myself, I also thought of a way to symbolize raising my shield of faith by acting out physically what I'm committing to do spiritually. I raise my right arm and hold out my hand like a shield. I then put up my thumb and declare, "God is who He says He is." I add my index finger and proclaim, "God can do what He says He can do." Adding my third finger, I say, "I am who God says I am." With my fourth finger I state, "I can do all things through Christ." My little finger completes the shield as I say, "God's Word is alive and active in me." I put an exclamation mark on the end of my five-statement pledge of faith with the simplest of sign language to the words "I'm believing God." With the index finger of that same hand, I point to my heart and say, "I'm." I point to my forehead and say, "believing" (because faith is always an exercise of the will, not the emotions). Then I point upward toward heaven and say, "God."

I practice this exercise in my house by myself, on walks with my dogs, in my car, at work with my staff, and anywhere else I can get away with it. As I make each statement, I can literally feel supernatural strength building within me. These statements are so ingrained in my mind that when Satan attacks me, I begin immediately tallying which statement he's trying to defy and I call it out. For instance, if I'm in need of a miracle, he might try to tempt me to believe God no longer performs wonders. I quickly go through my mental list of faith statements and call out number 2: "God can do what He says He can do!" Often the temptation to believe otherwise is instantaneously diffused. A second example involves an attack that has been highly successful for Satan . . . until recently. I've unfortunately provided the enemy a long list of past sins from which to accuse me. When he attacks me with condemnation now, I call out statement number 3, nice and loud: "I am who God says I am!" The results have been nothing less than transforming for me.

I've also taught this method to my classes in Houston, and if you want to experience a supernatural surge of God's Spirit, you ought to try proclaiming the five-statement pledge of faith with a few thousand others! At times when I'm in a public place where I'm not free to act it out and someone or something is trying to talk me out of faith, I do the simple sign language as I think to myself, "Say what you want, but I'm (pointing to my heart) believing (point to my head) God (pointing to heaven)." My spirit quickens just telling you about it.

Anytime someone makes fun of me or tells me I'm too radical and demonstrative for them, I have the same thought: "Beloved, I was once the most bound-up, defeated believer you've ever met, and now I'm a walking miracle experiencing the power of God. With all due respect, how's life going for you?" Sometimes God demands radical measures when He wants to bring about radical results. I may look silly, but to the glory of God alone, something's working. This woman should have been a lost cause.

Commit to say, write, or think your five-statement pledge of faith repeatedly over the time frame you choose with God. As for me, I think I'll declare it until I die. But even if you only repeat it for a number of weeks, I pray the practice will help put a new belief in your system.

2. *Increase your personal level of sanctification.* When the children of Israel were gathered on the water's edge with the Promised Land in sight, God gave Joshua the following instructions for their departure from the wilderness: "When you see the ark of the covenant of the LORD your God, and the priests, who are Levites, carrying it, you are to move out from your positions and follow it. Then you will know which way to go, since you have never been this way before" (Josh. 3:3–4). I am hoping God is about to take each of us to a place

with Him we've never been before. Even those who have already practiced present-active-participle belief in God haven't already arrived at every God-scheduled destination. If they had, He would have already swept them home to heaven. Our faith walk stops at His feet. Like the Israelites, we've still got places to go with God. And we've never been this way before.

Commit to say, write, or think your five-statement pledge of faith repeatedly over the time frame you choose with God.

The Israelites stood at the east bank of the Jordan prepared with faith, the absolute prerequisite for entering their Promised Land. The carcasses of the unbelieving generation littered the desert, and a people willing to follow a faith-filled leader took their places. As the flood-stage tide lapped at their sandals, Joshua gave them a second instruction to position them not only to take the land but to see God's wonders in the process. "Consecrate yourselves, for tomorrow the LORD will do amazing things among you" (Josh. 3:5). I love the definition of the Hebrew word *pala*, translated "amazing things" in the

NIV and "wonders" in the KJV. "To separate, distinguish; to be wonderful, do wonderful things; wondrous things, miracles. Used primarily with God as the subject, denoting the fact that He does things which are beyond the bounds of human powers or expectations."[2] In effect, God said to the Israelites, "If you set yourself apart to Me, I will distinguish Myself to you in ways more wonderful and miraculous than you have ever imagined."

I don't know about you, but I want to behold and experience any wonder God is willing to reveal to me. I not only want to have faith enough for God to grant me my Promised Land, I want to see amazing exploits of God while I'm there. If so, my life needs to be consecrated through an active pursuit of increasing personal holiness. Earlier I told you that I am asking God to do something amazing on your behalf during the course of your attentiveness to the message in this book. I have asked you to consider choosing a time frame with God to participate in three faith practices. The second faith practice is increasing your level of personal sanctification in a noticeable way over the designated length of time. The means is between God and you, but a few examples from the first group who joined me for a nine-week commitment might help get your mental wheels turning.

God has delighted me with the opportunity to minister to a diverse group of people that ranges from the completely unchurched to those in full-time ministry. Thankfully, we don't just "preach to the choir" at Living Proof Ministries. (Then again, I may as well point out that in my earlier years I committed some of my worst sins on Saturdays before singing in the choir on Sundays. I am one who believes the choir needs preaching to as much as anyone else.) Among our eclectic participants, some chose to stay out of nightclubs and not sleep around for nine weeks. This was a huge start and a significant sacrifice of accustomed lifestyle for some of them. Some who had drinking problems committed to give up alcohol. Others gave up watching R-rated movies and inappropriate television programs. Some who had never consistently read God's Word committed to a set time of daily Bible study and prayer. A number of participants gave up worldly music and replaced it with Christian contemporary and/or praise music for nine weeks. Others who were already observing significant spiritual disciplines fasted from a particular food or practice. Many gave up chocolate, for heaven's sake. Talk about commitment! The goal was choosing something significant enough to affect daily living.

We also wore a very effective reminder that I'd like to ask you to consider. The idea came from my daughter, Melissa. In middle school she and a small group of her friends made a pact that they would remain virgins until they were married. Then came high school. When Melissa was a sophomore, she learned that another of her friends had not been able to keep her commitment. These were not the kind of girls my mother's generation would have tagged "wild." They were simply darling and desirable. They were also vulnerable because of their unwillingness to make some black-and-white decisions and get out of the gray zone. The news of another casualty devastated Melissa and not only for her friend. She was terrified over the prospect that the same thing could happen to her because her walk was a little gray at that time as well. In sobs she grabbed her Bible, asked God to speak a word to her, and did something I don't recommend but appreciate God orchestrating. She threw open her Bible to a random page, closed her eyes, and pointed to a verse. In His merciful regard for her youth, this is the portion upon which her finger fell:

> The LORD said to Moses, "Speak to the Israelites and say to them: 'Throughout the generations to come you are to make tassels on the corners of your garments, with a blue cord on each tassel. You will have these tassels to look at and so you will remember all the commands of the LORD, that you may obey them and not prostitute yourselves by going after the lusts of your own hearts and eyes. Then you will remember to obey all my commands and will be consecrated to your God. I am the LORD your God, who brought you out of Egypt to be your God. I am the LORD your God.'" (Num. 15:37–41)

Melissa received the segment as a direct word from God, jerked open a drawer, found a blue ribbon, and marched resolutely down the stairs. With a tear-drenched face she pitched the ribbon to my husband, Keith, thrust out her right wrist, and said, "Tie it on me, Daddy!" He was only too happy to comply when he realized what it represented. "This way every time I'm tempted I'll only have to look as far as my wrist to remember my commitment." She wore it until it was a frazzled thread. By the time she took it off, she felt that the commitment was tied to her heart.

When I taught *Believing God* in my Houston Bible study, I urged each participant to wear some kind of thin blue cord on the right wrist throughout the journey. We saw everything from blue leather cords to blue beaded bracelets. My first class and I wore a simple strand of thick blue yarn. One young woman was so tenacious about her new faith walk that she wore it in her wedding that fell within our nine weeks. Like Melissa, we were greatly helped by a visible reminder of the commitment we had made to increase our personal sanctification. The sanctification bracelets were not meant to become yokes of legalistic bondage that had to be removed upon the first hint of infraction. Rather, they were meant to be reminders of a commitment and, if necessary, a call to return to it. Not a single participant so far has claimed the cords were ineffective.

Would you consider following suit? You will be surprised how motivational a visible reminder will be. After you choose your time frame and your means of practicing an increased level of sanctification, please get a durable thin blue cord of some kind and have someone, in Melissa's words, "tie it on" you. If you are like many of us who have taken this journey, this blue bracelet will end up representing something too important to discard when you complete your time. At the end of this book, I'll share what we did with our bracelets at the end of our nine weeks and ask you to consider something similar. Needless to say, one of the goals of this exercise is to be so blessed by the dividends of increased personal holiness that we cannot return to life as we knew it.

Jesus said, "My Father is always at his work to this very day, and I, too, am working." — John 5:17

Let's consider the third and final faith practice recommended for this journey:

3. *Journal Godstops.* In John 5:17, Jesus said, "My Father is always at his work to this very day, and I, too, am working." If you belong to Christ, I'd like to suggest that He and His Father are not only at work continually in the universe and among believers as a whole. They are always at work in and around you through

the third member of the Trinity. What you and I need is keener spiritual vision to behold some of Their activity and sense Their presence. We will be far more motivated to keep walking by faith with sharper spiritual sight. Ordinarily if I can perceive God at work, I feel like I can persevere through almost anything. In John 14:21, Jesus promised that He and His Father would disclose, or reveal, Themselves to those who loved Them and sought to walk in obedience. For those, a significant measure of spiritual vision is developed simply by watching.

I've asked God to work significantly in your life through the time frame you choose so that you will be all the more encouraged to practice action-verb faith in Him for the rest of your life. I believe the more we "see" God at work, the more we'll believe; and the more we believe, the more we're liable to see. As you participate with God in the increase of your faith and sanctification, God will undoubtedly be at significant work in your life. Our third faith practice is to watch. We will call the glimpses we catch of God at work "Godstops." The *stop* in Godstop is an acronym for "savoring the observable presence." God accomplishes so much that we don't

61

have eyes to see, but if He's willing to make some of His work and a measure of His presence observable, I want to stop all my distractions for a moment and see it. Don't you?

Recording Godstops is one effective way to develop keener spiritual sight. Throughout the time frame of your choice, I'd like to ask you to consider keeping a journal of small and large ways you see God at work. Record answered prayers and obvious interventions in dated entries. These entries do not need to be long and descriptive unless that's your style. Short sentences and phrases can be sufficient. The goal is to notice a God who is willingly, lovingly, and always at work in your life.

The stop in Godstop is an acronym for "savoring the observable presence."

These three faith practices become your personal investments in a great adventure with God. Let's downsize the chapter with a concluding recap. In order to invite God to put a fresh belief in your system, you're asked to choose a time frame for concentrating on a new walk of faith, and in that time frame willing participants are going to . . .

1. Practice raising your shield of faith by repeating the five-statement pledge of faith often, whether silently or aloud, until it is ingrained in your thinking.
2. Increase your personal level of sanctification in a specific way and wear some kind of blue cord as a reminder.
3. Keep a journal of Godstops — ways God is making His presence or activity observable.

Beloved, not only are these faith exercises doable, the attentiveness they require will affect an amazing renewal of the mind. What have you got to lose besides a load of defeat and doubt?

"Did God really say . . . ?"

If God said it, I want to believe it. If God gives it, I want to receive it. If God shows it, I want to perceive it. If Satan stole it, I want to retrieve it.

"I AM WHO I AM."

Exodus 3:14

Chapter Four

Believing God Is Who He Says He Is

So far we've learned that action-verb faith is our ticket to the Promised Land as well as our shield against opposition. In chapter 3, I introduced the following five-statement pledge of faith to help narrow down the broad concept of believing God into specifics we can get our spiritual arms around.

> **God is who He says He is.**
> **God can do what He says He can do.**
> **I am who God says I am.**
> **I can do all things through Christ.**
> **God's Word is alive and active in me.**

These five statements become a shield of faith to those who will allow them to penetrate the marrow of their belief systems. Recall for a moment the exercise I shared that demonstrates the practice of raising our shield of faith as we count off each statement on our fingers. The thumb principle is the most crucial because all the others hinge securely upon it. In physical terms none of us would argue that the thumb is the strongest appendage we have on our hand. If I want to grip something with my hand, I will fold my fingers around it, then secure it tightly with my thumb. We might say our hold on anything is only as secure as our thumbs. The thumb principle in our hand-raised shield of faith is statement number 1: God is who He says He is. In fact, He's either everything He says He is or He's a liar and unworthy of any faith at all. Thankfully, Scripture tells us that no deceit can be found in Him.

Over and over in Scripture, when God was about to move in the lives of His people or instruct them to reposition, He began with a reminder of who He was. A thumbs-up of sorts. The examples are numerous, but consider a few that directly relate to our Promised Land concept.

"I am the LORD, who brought you out of Ur of the Chaldeans to give you this land to take possession of it." (Gen. 15:7)

"I am God Almighty; walk before me and be blameless. I will confirm my covenant between me and you and will greatly increase your numbers." (Gen. 17:1–2)

"I am the God of your father, the God of Abraham, the God of Isaac and the God of Jacob. . . . I have indeed seen the misery of my people. . . . So I have come down to rescue them from the hand of the Egyptians and to bring them up out of that land into a good and spacious land." (Exod. 3:6–8)

God said to Moses, "I AM WHO I AM. This is what you are to say to the Israelites: 'I AM has sent me to you.' " (Exod. 3:14)

"Therefore, say to the Israelites: 'I am the LORD, and I will bring you out from under the yoke of the Egyptians. . . . And I will bring you to the land I swore with uplifted hand to give to Abraham, to Isaac and to Jacob. I will give it to you as a possession. I am the LORD.' " (Exod. 6:6, 8)

God knew that the most powerful driving force the children of Israel would have pressing them toward their earthly destiny was their certainty that the One who went before them was who He said He was.

Psalm 100:3 carries a powerful punch that can be easily missed in the poetry: "Know that the LORD is God." Know above all else that YHWH, our covenant Maker, is Elohiym, the God over all creation. In other words, you and I have got to know, not just hope or think, that the One who cut covenant with us through the torn flesh of Jesus Christ is the same One who sits upon the universe's throne, having spoken the worlds into existence. Surrounded by a society that spouts many gods but at best nobly agrees to equate them, you and I can know that the Lord is God. Hoping we're on the right track will never dig a deep enough path to follow to our Promised Lands. Beloved, we're not going anywhere of profound eternal significance until we know.

Christ practiced the same approach as He prepared His small band of followers to move into a land of promise beginning "in Jerusalem, and in all Judea and Samaria," then on to "the ends of the earth" (Acts 1:8). In Caesaria Philippi, Christ gathered His disciples around Him and asked them two vital questions that beg answers from us as well.

First, Christ asked, "Who do people say the Son of Man is?" (Matt. 16:13). Christ knew the potential power of popular opinion. As we consider the plausibility of our thumb principle — God is who He says He is — let's ask ourselves who the people around us say He is. The opinions of our culture span the entire spectrum from the belief that God does not exist all the way to the belief that God is who an inspired text says He is. In my estimation, atheism demands far more faith than theism, so I have never been significantly tempted to disbelieve in the existence of God. The evidence in His favor is overwhelming. I wouldn't have the energy for the endless rationalizations demanded to explain existence without Him. Genesis 1:1 begins with "In the beginning God created. . . ." Those who believe in a godless universe thus far can't even find a beginning to base their belief system upon. Psalm 14:1 says, "The fool says in his heart, 'There is no God.' "

Godless philosophies have not been my temptation. In my life experience the most dangerously influential opinions have been those held by intellectuals and scholars who profess Christianity but deny the veracity and present power of the Bible. To many, the Godhead exists, but they are not exactly who Scripture says they are. Neither do they do (or still do) what Scripture says they can do. The obvious brilliance of these scholars supported by a convincing list of degrees tempts those who wanted to believe God's Word to feel gullible and ignorant. The unspoken indictment is, "How could you be stupid enough to believe that?" Translation: "Did God really say . . . ?" Like Eve, we want to feel smart, so we end up making the stupidest decision of our lives. Nothing is more ignorant than choosing man's intelligence over God's.

Equally frightening is the potential for more humanly reasonable theologies to soothe and satisfy the follower's need to believe in a god, but the lesser god they're buying is not the God of Scripture. I don't think the biggest threat to our theology is humanism or the host of world religions. Our biggest threat is cut-and-paste Christianity. If man places his faith in a god he has recreated in his own image, has he placed his faith in God at all? And if not, how can such a man be saved?

On the other hand, a man or woman can believe enough of Scripture to accept Christ as Savior but refuse to accept who

He additionally says He is. I am Keith's wife, but what if Keith didn't accept that I was also the mother of his children? Or what if he didn't accept that I'd been called to be a servant of God? With a broken heart, I would wonder how he could say he knows me at all. The Bible describes a God who is a thousand things to His children. Thankfully, many churches and Christian institutes of higher learning teach the God of Scripture, but why do so many others default to a lesser-God theology?

If in our pursuit of knowledge God seems to have gotten smaller, we have been deceived.

I believe one reason is our arrogant determination to define God differently than He defines Himself. All human attempts to define God cannot help but minimize Him. We somehow want to neatly package God and make everything about Him explainable. We decide that what's not explainable is not plausible. We try to make God behave and fit into our textbooks. We want Him to calm down and not be so . . . God-ish. We decide we will only believe what we can humanly reconcile. Our pride and desperation to feel smart has made us unwilling to give the only human answer that exists to some theological questions: "I do not know. But I know that what He says is true even when I can't explain it or reconcile it with what has happened."

All attempts to take away the mystery and wonder that surround God leave Him something He is not. We cannot tame the Lion of Judah. There is a mystery, a wonder, and, yes, even a wildness about God we cannot take from Him. Nor would we want to if we could grasp the adventure of Him. If we can come up with a God we can fully explain, we have come up with a different God from the Bible's. We must beware of recreating an image of God that makes us feel better. Of this I'm certain: If in our pursuit of greater knowledge God seems to have gotten smaller, we have been deceived. I don't care how intelligent the deceiver seems or how well meaning and sincere his or her doctrine.

I can't count the mothers who have told me they were looking for a Christian school where their children could get "a good education and learn a little something about God." Be careful that your children are not learning that God is a little something. What kinds of theology are our institutions teaching? Flawless churches and Christian schools and universities don't exist because they are full of flawed people just like me, but we don't have to accept a lesser-God theology just because it's prevalent. We can make our own life's pursuit the God of Scripture, not just who man says He is. The beauty of the whole concept, of course, is that God is not changed one iota by who man says He is. Man's entire future, however, resides squarely upon its shoulders. Hence, Jesus' second question:

"Who do you say that I am?"

Who indeed? As we consider our thumb principle — God is who He says He is — we're wise to ask ourselves the question: Who do I say God is? Great wisdom is found in having the courage to take an inventory of how we have developed our present perceptions of God and how biblically accurate they are. Many people and factors can influence who we've come to believe God is: our grandparents, our parents, our upbringings, our teachers, our friends, our enemies, our experiences, our health, our hardships, our counselors or therapists, and every conceivable form of media. If we've attended church, our pastors and Bible teachers and their present or lacking authenticity have undoubtedly shaped our concept of God. Have those factors led us to believe God is who He says He is? Someone less? Or someone simply different? As we ask ourselves hard questions, keep in mind that faith unchallenged ordinarily remains unchanged.

Perhaps we'd all agree that who we believe God is greatly affects our eternal destinies, but I'd like to suggest that nothing has a greater effect on the quality of our lives and the fulfillment of our destinies on planet Earth. Scripture bulges with evidence not the least of which can be viewed in the verses that follow Christ's paramount question to His disciples:

"Who do you say I am?"

Simon Peter answered, "You are the Christ, the Son of the living God."

Jesus replied, "Blessed are you, Simon son of Jonah, for this was not revealed to you by man, but by my Father in heaven. And I tell you that you are Peter, and on this rock I will build my church, and the gates of Hades will not overcome it. I will give you the keys of the kingdom of heaven; whatever you bind on earth will be bound in heaven, and whatever you loose on earth will be loosed in heaven." (Matt. 16:15–20)

Though Christ would build His church on the foundation of the apostles' testimonies, I don't think Peter understood Christ to say that He would build His entire church on His star pupil alone (compare 1 Cor. 3:11). In the Greek New Testament the word used for Peter is *Petros,* usually meaning "a stone, a piece or fragment" of a bigger boulder. The word used for the "rock" upon which Christ would build His church is *Petra,* usually meaning "a massive rock or cliff." Is it possible Christ was pointing to Himself as the massive rock upon which He'd build His church and Peter as the chip off the Block whose testimony of Christ would pour the foundation for many? I'm not sure exactly what Christ meant, but clearly Peter was assigned tremendous position and responsibility in the kingdom. There is no mistaking, "I will give you the keys of the kingdom of heaven" (Matt. 16:19).

In ancient Eastern customs, the master or king over an estate gave keys to his possessions to a trusted steward to dispense those possessions according to his master's wishes. Joseph is an Old Testament example of a trusted steward. Though he had tremendous responsibility, the kingdom was built upon the pharaoh, whose solitary rule was uncontested. As Joseph proved tenacious and trustworthy, the pharaoh in effect gave him a set of keys to dispense kingdom provisions (like grain) according to his master's wishes. Consider the parallel: Joseph could be trusted because he knew the pharaoh was who he said he was. He also knew above all that God was who He said He was and that His sovereign authority was at work.

In our paradigm, Peter received and would fulfill his earthly destiny first and foremost because he believed Christ was who God revealed Him to be. Do you see the undeniable link between believing God is who He says He is and fulfilling our God-ordained destinies? The original Greek terminology in Matthew 16:19 implies another concept that will prove vital to our faith walk. Not only did Christ promise Peter the keys of the kingdom, He said, "Whatever you bind on earth will be bound in heaven, and whatever you loose on earth will be loosed in heaven."

We hear lots of things in today's Christian culture about "binding and loosing." I want to know what the phrase means because, frankly, whatever God is willing to empower us to do in this world system, I want to do. I don't want to miss anything. In order to gain some insight into Christ's intention, we have to talk verb tenses again. In Matthew 16:19, both words "binding" and "loosing" are perfect passive participles, which could more literally be interpreted, "having been bound" and "having been loosed."

The tone of this interpretation is expressed beautifully in the Amplified Bible: "I will give you the keys of the kingdom of heaven; and whatever you bind (declare to be improper and unlawful) on earth must be what is already bound in heaven; and whatever you loose (declare lawful) on earth must be what is already loosed in heaven."

God doesn't work for us;
we work for God.

If this interpretation of the verb tense is accurate, we still have no reason to be disappointed. In actuality the concept has much broader and far more wonderful implications from this standpoint. The principle implied is congruent with the essence of the prayer Jesus taught His disciples:

"Your will be done on earth as it is in heaven" (Matt. 6:10). Give the concept some thought with me for a moment. Why in the world would God give carte blanche permission to human flesh and blood to bind and loose whatever he (the believer) interpreted was wrong or right? Take Peter for instance. Just a few verses after Jesus proclaimed Peter's future place of authority, Peter rebuked Jesus for having the audacity to suggest He would "suffer many things at the hands of the elders, chief priests and teachers of the law, and that he must be killed" (Matt. 16:21). Had Peter had his way, he would have bound the cross and unknowingly loosed the world from any hope of salvation.

God doesn't sit upon His throne saying, "Oops, I wouldn't have done that, but now that you have, I guess I'll go with it." Remember, God doesn't work for us; we work for God. If God had given me my way, I would have bound and loosed three or four husbands by the time I was twenty-five. His desire is to see believers bind and loose what He wants for them. Beloved, God has made so much available to us. He foreordained a perfect plan for each of our lives and has stored up immeasurable blessing that He longs for His children to loose by faith. David understood the concept when he sang, "How great is your goodness, which you have stored up for those who fear you, which you bestow in the sight of men" (Ps. 31:19). The terminology David used doesn't sound like a promise intended for heaven alone. "In the sight of men" intimates the transference of some heavenly goods onto earthly sod.

God has invited us to participate in kingdom affairs, and, yes, even kingdom authority under the rule of His righteous will. He extends staggering power to those willing to think with the mind of Christ rather than the mind of man. God would also empower His children to bind untold evils and strongholds if we'd believe Him and cooperate with Him. Talk about abundant life! Where does this kind of existence begin? With biblical answers to the pivotal question, "Who do you say that I am?"

God is looking for stewards who are willing to bind their own unbelief in the mighty name of Jesus and loose a fresh anointing of faith onto the topsoil of earth. Are you game?

"LORD, I have heard of your fame: I stand in awe of your deeds, O LORD. Renew them in our day, in our time make them known."

Habakkuk 3:2

Chapter Five

Believing God Can Do What He Says He Can Do

We concluded our previous chapter with a deeper understanding of what we can bind and loose as Christ's disciples in this generation. Our second statement in our pledge of faith places a titanic challenge before us to bind our unbelief and loose a fresh anointing of faith. Recall statement 1:

God is who He says He is.

Compare statement 2:

God can do what He says He can do.

> God can do what He says He can do
> precisely because He is who He says
> He is.

I'm convinced most of us tend to accept the first statement in our pledge more readily than the second. We less quickly assume that God is able — or is, perhaps more pointedly willing — to do what He says He can do. Ironically, however, God can do what He says He can do precisely because He is who He says He is. Most of the biblical titles for God inseparably connect who He is to what He can do. For instance: as Savior, He saves; as Deliverer, He delivers; as Redeemer, He redeems; as Master, He assumes authority; as Bread of Life, He provides; and as Almighty, He exerts divine strength.

Before God insisted on calling me to fresh faith six years ago, I certainly believed He was who He said He was, but I was much less sure that He still works miracles in our day. I had been taught that God does not work many miracles today because we live in a different time period on the kingdom calendar. Not only did God prove me wrong, I think He had a fairly good time turning my neatly compartmentalized belief system upside down. He seems to like saying, "Oh, yes I will" to the "Oh, no He won'ts." God doesn't at all mind proving His own people wrong to prove His Word right. He never works contrary to Scripture, but the issue at hand is the stronghold of unbelief in the church concerning biblical acts of God.

I have a friend who has struggled for many years with extreme highs and lows, a malady her doctor later diagnosed as bipolar disorder. From what she has described, I'm not sure today's church couldn't be diagnosed with a spiritual case of something similar. The primary difference is that the body of Christ feels two extremes at once. Two diametrically opposed teachings exist on the subject of faith and miracles, making us one body with a divided mind. For our purposes we'll call our two extremes *cessationism* and *sensationalism*. The magnetic power pulling Christians to one pole or the other is overwhelming. So is man's insecure desire to be doctrinally black or white, one extreme or another. We find great security in *always* and *never;* hence, our bipolar existence.

Simply put, cessationism teaches that more dramatic miracles have ceased in our day. Sensationalism teaches that the whole point of belief is miracles. The former says God wants nothing to do with miracles in our day, and the latter depicts God as one big miracle machine. I love the body of Christ and have dear friends and people I respect on all sides of the spectrum. My complaint is not people. My complaint is the tendency of people, like me, to be drawn toward doctrinal extremes. Frankly, I've got a crick in my neck from watching them both, and I beg God for a biblical center.

In the Gospels, Christ called those without faith to believe in miracles an "unbelieving and perverse generation" (Luke 9:41). On the other hand, He called those who focused entirely on miracles a "wicked and adulterous generation" (Matt. 16:4). If the body of Christ in our generation is set on being bipolar, our choice is whether we'd rather be an unbelieving and perverse generation or a wicked and adulterous generation. Hmmmmm. Not good choices. They both have one thing in common, however: they are severely experiential. Sensationalism seeks an experience, and cessationism believes only what it personally sees and experiences. Sensationalism suggests that everything possible is also probable, while cessationism accepts only the presently probable as the presently possible.

Either extreme can be wildly offensive to God. Perhaps the most serious offense of sensationalism is its overwhelming tendency to be man-centered rather than God-centered, prioritizing what God can do over who He is. The reason Christ could dub miracle cravers as adulterous is because they worshipped God's wonders more than God Himself. Equally idolatrous, sensationalism suggests we can believe God as long as He does what we tell Him to do, as if we were the potter and God the clay. Before you decide sensationalism is the worse offender of the two extremes, consider the wages of cessationalism. It not only cheats the believer of the pleasure and coinciding rewards of God that come to those who exercise faith (Heb. 11:6), it also severely undercuts hope. Look at the close scriptural association between faith and hope:

- "Now faith is being sure of what we hope for" (Heb. 11:1).
- "Through him you believe in God, who raised him from the dead and glorified him, and so your faith and hope are in God" (1 Pet. 1:21).
- "Against all hope, Abraham in hope be-

lieved [exercised faith] and so became the father of many nations" (Rom. 4:18).

- "And now these three remain: faith, hope and love" (1 Cor. 13:13).

Hypercessationist doctrines can knock the feet of hope from under us. Beloved, no one, no matter how brilliant, persuasive, or credentialed, should have the right to take away our hope. The God we serve is able (Dan. 3:17). Everything is possible (Mark 9:23). Nothing is impossible (Luke 1:37). We can always hope and pray diligently for a miracle. If, in God's sovereignty, He chooses to accomplish His purposes another way, let it not be that we have not because we asked not (James 4:2) or that we have not because we believed not (Matt. 9:29).

Second Corinthians 1:20 tells us that "no matter how many promises God has made, they are 'Yes' in Christ." Christ gave His life so God could say yes to the fulfillment of His promises in the lives of believing mortals. Therefore, I am utterly convinced that any *no* an earnestly seeking child of God receives from the Throne is for the sake of a greater *yes,* whether realized on earth or in heaven. A present-active-participle believer will see miracles, all right. Sometimes the greater miracle may be abundant life, redemption, ministry, and exceeding harvest after a no we felt we wouldn't survive. If you dare to believe and you don't get your miracle, God has a greater one planned. Stay tuned. If what you desperately need or deeply desire is founded in the Word of God, don't let anyone tell you that God can't . . . or that He undoubtedly won't.

"And he will be called Wonderful" (Isa. 9:6). Full of wonders. Remove the wonders from God, and you can no longer call Him wonderful. Has God ceased to be wonderful today?

In *C. S. Lewis: Readings for Meditation and Reflection*, editor Walter Hooper offers some of the author's thoughts pertaining to our subject: "Do not attempt," [Lewis] advised, "to water Christianity down. There must be no pretense that you can have it with the Supernatural left out. So far as I can see Christianity is precisely the one religion from which the miraculous cannot be separated."[3]

Though my ministry is joyfully interdenominational, I attend and serve a church that is part of a denomination. Our denomination is known for many wonderful things, such as emphasis on evangelism and world missions, but we don't have a wide reputation for believing God for the dramatically miraculous. I cannot express how thankful and thrilled I am to report that my precious church — as well as many others — is an exception to any such stereotype. One reason I know without a doubt God still performs miracles is because I have seen them within my own praying congregation. God has undoubtedly healed several people I know personally of chronic and terminal diseases as well as intervened in countless ways that could only be divine. At the same time, we have also bent the knee to God when He worked differently in the lives of other loved ones, bringing me to my next statement: I won't argue that the church as a whole sees a fraction of the miracles described in the Gospels and Acts.

Many might say that miracles in the New Testament were solely for the purpose of authenticating the messengers and the message; therefore, since the church is established and Scripture complete, they are no longer necessary. The varied circumstances under which miracles were performed, however, suggest that authentication could not have been the sole purpose of miracles. Christ also performed miracles simply out of compassion. In Nain, He raised the son of a widow from the dead because "his heart went out to her" (Luke 7:13). Luke 5:17 also suggests that other times Jesus performed miracles because "the power of the Lord was present" or we might say "creating an environment" to do so.

I don't doubt that a host of reasons exist why the present body of Christ witnesses fewer miracles and wonders than the early church, but for our purposes I wish to highlight two. The first one is a personal conviction that is surely obvious by this point of the book. I fear we are a dreadfully unbelieving generation, particularly the portion of us in the prosperous West. Reports of miracles come out of many Third World countries where all they seem to have is their faith. The reason I can spot unbelieving believers pretty readily is because, as they say, it takes one to know one. I was at the front of the line for many years of my adult life. We are caught in a tragic cycle. We believe little because we see little, so we see little and continue to believe little. It's time we dumped this wobbling cycle for a form of transportation that really gets us somewhere. In order to make the trade-in, we must cease to accept the visible as the possible and start believing what God says over what man sees.

The second reason we see fewer miracles may reflect an ounce of what some cessationists weigh by the ton. Though I know wonders haven't ceased because I've seen and experienced them, I won't argue that according to His sovereignty, God may have greater purpose and higher priorities for more widespread miracles in some generations and geographies than others. My argument is that we could use some profound works of God in our here and now, and He may just be waiting for us to muster up some corporate belief and start asking Him. Even many of my cessationist friends believe that a day of miracles and wonders will come again before the end of times. My questions are simple: Why can't that be now? Must it wait? Could God even now be waiting for a revival of faith? He is the Initiator, the very Author, of faith (Heb. 12:2). Could this restlessness and dissatisfaction we feel in our souls be Christ initiating and authorizing a new day of awakened faith and outpoured Spirit? Oh, God, let it be. Please don't misunderstand that believing God only involves believing Him for dramatic miracles. If we don't include believing Him for the miraculous, however, can you imagine the tragedy of all we could miss?

We are certainly not the first generation missing widespread wonders. Gideon's generation found itself under terrible enemy oppression. They hid in strongholds and fell into an ineffectiveness far removed from their promised position. Sound familiar? Impoverished, the Israelites cried out to the Lord for help. Check out what happened next.

"When the angel of the LORD appeared to Gideon, he said, 'The LORD is with you, mighty warrior.' "

" 'But sir,' Gideon replied, 'if the LORD is with us, why has all this happened to us? Where are all his wonders that our fathers told us about?' " (Judg. 6:12–13). In His great mercy God even gave Gideon's faith lots of evidence and encouragement on which to grow. He simply wanted him to show a little cooperation. A mustard seed, we might say. The rest is history. The precedent God set in Gideon's generation offers me no small encouragement in the publishing of this message. Even if the masses do not welcome God to pour out a fresh anointing of faith upon His church, He can still perform wonders through a small army.

Generations after Gideon's encounter with the God of wonders, God's people searched once again for missing miracles. The psalmist asked a critical question in Psalm 77:7: "Will [the Lord] never show his favor again?" Follow the trail of his thoughts as he continues in verses 10–14:

> Then I thought, "To this I will
>   appeal:
> the years of the right hand of the
>   Most High."
> I will remember the deeds of the
>   LORD;
> yes, I will remember your miracles
>   of long ago.
> I will meditate on all your works
> and consider all your mighty deeds.
> Your ways, O God, are holy.
> What god is so great as our God?
> You are the God who performs
>   miracles;
> you display your power among the
>   peoples.

Read it again: "You are the God who performs miracles." Present tense.

The Sons of Korah echo the sentiment in Psalm 44:1: "We have heard with our ears, O God; our fathers have told us what you did in their days, in days of long ago." Like us, they had heard with their ears, but they were desperate to see with their eyes. So are we! And so is our world. Psalm 74 intimates that when God withheld wonders, His thinking people assumed something was wrong (as did Gideon), and the wise rightly searched for the disconnection. The ninth and eleventh verses say, "We are given no miraculous signs; no prophets are left, and none of us knows how long this will be. . . . Why do you hold back your hand, your right hand?" The twenty-second verse pleads, "Rise up, O God, and defend your cause."

If in reality we are seeing few wonders of God in the midst of His people and through His people, shouldn't we as well inquire why? Are we not equally desperate? Is God no longer willing to intervene miraculously and wondrously in our behalf? We are surrounded by a dying and depraved world, mounting violence and threat of mass destruction, disease, plague, enticing false religion, and a surging fury of satanic assault and seduction. We are desperate for the wonders and miracles of God. We need Him to show His mighty arm and tell the world that He is alive, active, and very much with us. We are told churches are in terrible decline. Many pastors and leaders are depressed. Oppressed. Throngs of clueless people encircle us. We need more than the best programs and planning can accomplish. In fact, we need more than we even have the courage or imagination to ask.

Oh, that the church would fall on its face and cry out the words the prophet Habakkuk cried: "LORD, I have heard of your fame; I stand in awe of your deeds, O LORD. Renew them in our day, in our time make them known" (3:2).

The time has come for the church to appeal to the "years of the right hand of the Most High" (Ps. 77:10).

"Did I tell you that if you believed, you would see the glory of God?"

John 11:40

Chapter Six

Believing God for His Best

I want so many things for my children. I shamelessly ask God to bless them and show them favor. I actively ask Him to grant them good health; lots of joy; long-lasting romance with their life mates; laughter; healthy, happy children; and lots of good friends. I also have no problem asking God if He might purpose them to live in fairly close proximity so that I can rock my grandbabies often and, when they're older, take them to the park and, when they're even older, shoot a few baskets with them. Knowing that my children have surrendered their lives to ministry and all the things that could mean, I'm not shy to ask for them to be delivered from constant financial struggles and disillusionment with church work. Those requests are important to me. I feel no conviction of sin over the temporal nature of some of those petitions.

> All that will matter forever and ever in our heavenly state is the glory that came to God through our lives.

As much as I hope God grants my children each of those things, they represent my B list. You can bet I have an A list. I want my children to love God. I tell them often that a passionate love for God and a constant awareness of His grace is their heritage and that neither mediocrity nor legalism has a place in our family line. I want my children to love God's Word and discover the life, healing, and power within it. I want my children to love people and treat them with compassion and kindness. But more than anything on earth — tears fill my eyes as I write these words — I want glory to come to God through my children. I want a thousand things for them and ask without hesitation, but I want nothing more than God to be glorified. Life is just a breath. All that will matter forever and ever in our heavenly state is the glory that came to God through our lives.

Thus, God and I have this deal. I know He has endless resources and that I will never ask more than He can supply, so I feel free to ask anything I desire for my loved ones, then I try to be careful to jump up and down with a grateful heart for all He grants. At the same time, God knows my absolute priorities for them. Therefore, if something on my A list temporarily or even permanently (ouch!) might have to cancel out something on my B list, so be it. I'll bend the knee, however painfully, because I am most desperate for them to know and experience the truest of all riches. Still, I'll continue to ask for A and B and a host of Cs, like "Lord, Amanda and Curt really want that summer pass to Six Flags Astroworld. Would you help them afford it?"

God has the power and authority to grant anything on a list A–Z. All the resources of heaven and earth belong to Him. Even if something I've asked for my children necessitated a miracle, without hesitation I believe God could accomplish it. When I'm in heaven, however, I am certain that I will esteem the greatest miracle of all being godly offspring who brought Him glory from such formerly sinful and enslaved parents. God has performed miracles in my behalf even to the degree of a physical healing, but to date, Keith and I consider the greatest miracle of all to be the way He is transforming our family line.

"If you, then, though you are evil, know how to give good gifts to your children, how much more will your Father in heaven give good gifts to those who ask him!" (Matt. 7:11). If we, being comparatively evil parents, have priorities concerning what we believe to be the best life has to offer for our children, would we be surprised to think that God does too? Ours is a God of priorities. Might He have an A and a B list? I wouldn't be surprised if He has a list for each of us stretching all the way from alpha to omega. After all, "How great is your goodness, which you have stored up for those who fear you, which you bestow in the sight of men on those who take refuge in you" (Ps. 31:19). Scripture is replete with God's bountiful desires for us, but He also clearly knows what He desires most to accomplish not only in each believer, but in each generation.

What does prioritizing have to do with miracles and our second statement of faith? At times, almost everything. God can do what He says He can do. And, yes, with all my heart I believe He is willing to perform outstanding miracles in our generation as we increase our faith. I have and undoubtedly will continue to ask God to perform wonders on behalf of my loved ones and those whom I serve. At the same time I also believe that the greatest miracle of all is glory coming to the Father through mortal creatures. If God can gain glory through the miracle I've requested, hallelujah! If I don't get my miracle but God gets greater glory, I choose to believe I received the greater miracle with the most eternal dividends. Undoubtedly and ultimately we will be most blessed when God is most glorified. This concept is what I called "the greater yes" in our previous chapter.

Don't dare lose heart and think you already see the handwriting on the wall: "I may as well accept that God will be most glorified by my not getting the miracle I so desperately want or think I need." Check out Scripture! God was often glorified through the miracle that blessed temporally as well. To Martha, who was grieving the death of her brother, Jesus said, "Did I not tell you that if you believed, you would see the glory of God?" (John 11:40). And He revealed that glory by raising her brother from the dead. Don't assume to know how God will be most glorified. Ask for the miracle, then let our sovereign, wise, and long-range planning God measure the glory and determine if a greater one is at stake.

Recently I got to serve with my friend

Jennifer Rothschild at Focus on the Family. I sat on the front row fighting back tears as I marveled over the miracle God has performed in her life. Actually, she and her parents asked Him for a different kind of miracle. They asked that she be healed of the blindness that began to overtake her in elementary school. He did not. Instead, He performed a greater miracle. She is a gorgeous and gifted singer and musician. As if that's not unfair enough, she also speaks like an angel. She is the essence of grace and beauty. You might say she has it all . . . except her physical sight. Mark my word, Jennifer Rothschild is going to be used by God powerfully in our generation. She writes and also teaches Bible studies on video. Much glory is coming to God through her life. Still, Jennifer makes no bones about it. She would very much like to have her sight. The complications of Jennifer's blindness are endless as she raises two boys she cannot physically see. Yet in eternity we'll have plenty of chances to ask Jennifer if she would have traded in her blindness for a life of mediocrity and greater independence from God. I think we can expect her to say no. She cooperated with God and got the greater yes.

In chapter 5 I told you that I don't have

difficulty believing that God in His sovereignty could prioritize miracles and wonders in some generations and eras more than others. I want to share with you what I think He may be prioritizing in our generation and in those occupying the space between the establishment of the New Testament church and the end of times. I do not desire to be dogmatic on this point. I offer food for thought on the table of a familiar meal.

At the Last Supper, Christ introduced a term with revolutionary implications. As He raised the cup, He said, "This cup is the new covenant in my blood, which is poured out for you" (Luke 22:20). The New Testament books of 2 Corinthians and Hebrews expound upon this new covenant and compare it to the old. Consider a few vital contrasts:

- The old covenant was "of the letter," meaning the letter of the law. The new covenant is "of the Spirit" (2 Cor. 3).
- The letter of the old covenant was written on "tablets of stone." The letter of the new covenant is written on "tablets of human hearts" (2 Cor. 3). Hebrews 10:16 says, "This is the covenant I will make with them after that time, says the Lord. I will put my laws in their hearts, and I will write them on their minds."

You and I are under the new covenant. If we understood the fullness of the implications, we'd shout "Glory!" And indeed that would be the key word. We look upon the lives of people like Moses and wish we had such manifestations and revelations of divine presence, yet 2 Corinthians 3:9–10 says, "If the ministry that condemns men is glorious, how much more glorious is the ministry that brings righteousness! For what was glorious has no glory now in comparison with the surpassing glory." So, you see, if we really comprehended the meaning, we'd not only shout "Glory!" We'd shout, "Surpassing glory!"

For our purposes I want to center on one primary difference between the covenants and what 2 Corinthians 3 refers to as the "ministry" of those covenants. The ministry of the old covenant was in many ways primarily external in nature with secondarily internal repercussions. The law was written upon external and visible tablets of stone. God manifested His glory in many physical and visible forms, such as manna, a cloudy pillar by day, and fire by night. Those who chose to be internally changed by what they saw and experienced were.

In important contrast, the new covenant

became a primarily internal work with wonderful external manifestations. It was and is the ministry of the Spirit to human hearts and minds. The ministry of the new covenant is the ministry of the Holy Spirit not just around, upon, and with believers but also inside believers. Jesus spoke of the Holy Spirit to His disciples when He said, "he lives with you and will be in you" (John 14:17). Please meditate on the profound difference between the words "with" and "in." The difference made a band of fumbling scaredy-cats in the Gospel records unparalleled powerhouses in the book of Acts and beyond. The same work of the Spirit is applied to us in 2 Corinthians 4:7: "But we have this treasure in jars of clay to show that this all-surpassing power is from God and not from us." You see, the new covenant is primarily an inward work with glorious outward manifestations.

Thankfully, God can often perform a miracle in our circumstances and in our hearts and minds simultaneously.

What does this have to do with priorities? I believe God's greatest priorities in the age between the establishment of the New Testament (or covenant) church and the latter days is internal. One of the chief responsibilities of the bride of Christ in this age is to "make herself ready" for Jesus Christ, her Bridegroom (Rev. 19:7). Christ will return for a pure bride, a state of being that necessitates deep, internal works. God's eyes are fastened with eternal intentions on the inner man. That's why sometimes God may prioritize performing a miracle on our hearts and minds over a miracle concerning our circumstances.

I shared this view with a knowledgeable friend who responded with a good question: "But, Beth, aren't you saying what cessationists basically believe anyway?" I can't answer for anyone else, but having been a cessationist for so long, I have experienced a dramatic difference between my old approach and my new. Before, I may have hoped for a miracle, but I can't say I ever expected one. I treated a miracle as a last hope. Quite often now a miracle might be my first hope, prayer, and anxious expectation; but if I don't receive it, I assume God has a more inward agenda. The difference has been like night and day. I have witnessed God's miraculous intervention more times than I can count and a greater sense of peace and confidence when I haven't.

Thankfully, God can often perform a

miracle in our circumstances and in our hearts and minds simultaneously. I'd like to suggest that from His eternal standpoint, however, the works He desires to accomplish within us may take precedence over those He desires to work around us. Ephesians 3:20–21 expresses this concept beautifully. We who are familiar with these passages often speak of God doing "immeasurably more than we could ask or think." But take a look at the context and note where He desires to do these kinds of works most:

"Now to him who is able to do immeasurably more than all we ask or imagine, according to his power that is at work within us, to him be glory in the church and in Christ Jesus throughout all generations, for ever and ever! Amen."

"According to His power that is at work" where? "Within us."

The new covenant far surpasses the old in numerous ways, but I would be remiss not to mention an element of it that we tend to view negatively. In reality, ignorance is rarely bliss because not knowing the biblical facts does not render them void. So, at the risk of disappointing you, here goes: Suffering has an undeniable role in the New Testament and under the new covenant. If you're like me, many of the miracles you seek are toward the avoidance of further difficulty, pain, or suffering. Nothing is wrong with that. We have a blessed biblical precedent to ask repeatedly for thorns to be removed before we accept them as God's sovereign appointment for a greater work (2 Cor. 12:8–9). Understanding the role of suffering, however, helps us understand a little more readily why God is able to perform a miracle He may not choose to perform.

Priorities.

If we are accurate in our estimation of the inward priority of the new covenant, we might assume that no one will completely forego suffering. Neither will those who don't know Christ, I might add. Unfortunately, no one in this present world system foregoes suffering. It is a compulsory part of human existence in a terribly fallen world. The difference for believers is that our suffering need never be in vain. Few things have comparable potential to be used by God for excellent internal works with glorious external ramifications.

In 2 Corinthians, the same book that speaks so readily of our position under the new covenant, Paul explains: "Therefore we do not lose heart. Though outwardly we are wasting away, yet inwardly we are being renewed day by day. For our light and momentary troubles are achieving for us an eternal glory that far outweighs them all" (2 Cor. 4:16–17).

Priorities.

Romans 8:17 says, "Now if we are children, then we are heirs — heirs of God and co-heirs with Christ, if indeed we share in his sufferings in order that we may also share in his glory." Thankfully, Paul tells us in the very next verse that he doesn't consider any present sufferings to be remotely comparable with the glory God will reveal "in us."

Priorities.

First Peter 1:7 speaks of trials: "These have come so that your faith — of greater worth than gold, which perishes even though refined by fire — may be proved genuine and may result in praise, glory and honor when Jesus Christ is revealed."

Knowing the truth about God,
His unceasing ability to
perform miracles, . . .
frees me up to believe Him more.

Priorities.

The list could go on and on. New Testament Scripture stacks up too much evidence for us to claim that suffering is never within the plan of our sovereign God, whether through His perfect or permissive will. Do the new covenant priorities of inward works and the role of suffering discourage me from asking and believing God for miracles? Hardly! And I'll tell you why. Knowing the truth always sets us free (John 8:32). Knowing the truth about God, His unceasing ability to perform miracles, and the truth about the undeniable role of suffering under the new covenant only frees me up to believe Him more. Why? Because I'm freed from what scares me, and many of you, most about getting out there and believing God. We're scared half to death that He won't come through for us, dignify us with a yes, and prove faithful. Or that we'll prove to be failures at having enough belief for Him to bless with a miracle. If I'm convinced that God really loves me and has certain priorities for me that may take precedence at times, then I am "safe" to walk by faith. I am freed to know that my God is huge and my God is able and that if I don't get what I asked, if I'll cooperate, I'll get something bigger. I'm going to believe Him to do anything His Word says He can, then if He chooses not to, I don't have to assume . . .

- He doesn't like me.
- He doesn't answer my prayers like He does others'.
- He hardly knows I'm alive.
- He can't do it.
- He's never willing to do it.
- I didn't have enough faith.
- I wavered for a split second.
- I have that sin in my past.
- I'm a failure.
- I've made a fool of myself.

Instead, I get to know that a greater yes is in progress, and I can count on the bigger miracle.

Beloved, we are safe with God. We are safe to believe Him for miracles. I think the time is also hastening on the kingdom calendar when God's agenda will include greater miracles, signs, and wonders as He ushers in the last days. Whether or not you and I see those days and plentiful wonders, we are free to believe that God is who He says He is and can do what He says He can do. Neither His dignity nor ours is at stake. Neither are we insignificant nor God incompetent. We are safe with God because we *are* His priority.

In the meantime, if we want to be filled with faith and behold some wonders, we are wise to avoid giving in to two temptations: judging and arguing. Whatever we do, we must avoid judging someone else for a weaker or lesser faith. I have enough fear of God in me to know that I will likely be tested on the very things I've judged about others (Rom. 2:1). I've experienced exactly this kind of repercussion in the past, and my failure to pass some of those tests helps cure me from the habit.

If we want to experience God's blessing, we don't want to judge those of lesser faith. On the other hand, neither do we want to be negatively influenced by those of lesser faith. Mark 9 records an interesting interchange between Christ and His disciples after some of them were unable to cast a demon from a tormented child. Keep in mind that Jesus had empowered His disciples to perform this very act, yet they were unable to do so in this circumstance. Mark 9:14 says, "When [Jesus and a few of His disciples] came to the other disciples, they saw a large crowd around them and the teachers of the law arguing with them." The inability of the disciples was reported to Jesus, but before He reprimanded His chosen appointees for their unbelief, He asked them a critical question, "What are you arguing with [the teachers of the law] about?" (v. 16).

I am convinced that the argument the disciples had with the educated, dignified teachers of the law diminished their faith so drastically that they were unable to do one of the very things they had been empowered to do. If you want to be full of faith, don't argue with a legalist! Love them. Serve side by side with them if God wills. Don't judge them. And don't argue with them! Unbelief is highly contagious. Frivolous arguments can dilute spiritual truths into human logic. Nothing is logical about miracles. To the degree that we debate matters of faith, we could find ourselves drained of it. We are not called to debate faith but to do it. To be nouns turned into verbs. Presently. Actively.

Keep seeking. Keep believing. I am convinced that the pure-hearted, faith-filled petitioner is going to behold a miracle. Whether lesser or greater, temporal or eternal, wonders never cease.

"Did I not tell you that if you believed, you would see the glory of God?" (John 11:40). Count on it every time.

"Who am I, that I should go . . . ?"

Exodus 3:11

Chapter Seven

Believing You Are
Who God Says You Are

> **God is who He says He is.**
> **God can do what He says He can do.**

I pray that these two statements are being ingrained deeper and deeper within our belief systems. God desires "truth in the innermost being" (Ps. 51:6 NASB). May He invade even our subconscious minds with His Word.

Of all five statements in our pledge of faith, none present me the unrelenting challenge of the third:

> **I am who God says I am.**

This truth unearths emotion in me every time I say it because I am reminded of the journey I've had to take to believe it. Believing I am who God says I am necessities choosing what God says over what I feel more than any other faith challenge I face. For the most part, I have a messy conglomeration of early childhood victimization and a long-term history of defeat to thank for my deep insecurity and uncertainty. Actually, *self-torment* would be a better word for it. I suppose it's the residuals of a formerly self-destructive nature. Whatever it is, it waves like a red flag to the enemy: "Hit her right here! This is where she's weakest. Aim here!"

I want so much to be a woman of faith. In fact, I'd give just about anything to be a woman God could characterize by her faith since nothing pleases Him more (Heb. 11:6). So, if I'm really serious about believing God, I have to believe God about me. No small challenge. Let's just say I haven't exactly been a low maintenance project for Him. I would tell you that God has to be omnipotent to have kept me out of the ditch as long as He has, but He was also omnipotent through my tumbles. I was the problem. Goodness knows, God has done His part. At lunch today I told my staff with much laughter that if I die suddenly, my gravestone might appropriately offer this insight into my departure: "God got tired." I require lots of work. That's one reason I have a little hang-up with statement three. I tend to want to rewrite it, "I strive to be who God says I am." Nope. That's not what the Word says. It says I'm already who God says I am. If you have received Jesus as your Savior, so are you. We'll get a little glimpse of what that means in a moment.

I wonder about all those historical figures listed in the Hebrews 11 hall of faith. Do you think some of them had a little trouble believing they were who God said they were? I can't answer for all of them, but Moses is a dead giveaway. The first question he asked God after he heard His voice from the burning bush was, "Who am I, that I should go to Pharaoh and bring the Israelites out of Egypt?" (Exod. 3:11). Later in the conversation Moses had the ire-raising audacity to respond to his call, "O Lord, please send someone else to do it" (Exod. 4:13).

Moses had his own reasons for resisting his call and his new identity as God's servant, but we share at least one in common. He, too, had terrible sin in his past. I wonder about Joshua, though. Scripture paints him as a mighty warrior and a true worshipper who tarried in the presence of God. We read no history of failure. At first we might assume he was confident and ready for anything; but immediately following God's official command for his life, the first chapter of Joshua could intimate something to the contrary. Repetitions are usually telling in the Bible, and within a few short verses, God told Joshua to "be strong and courageous" no less than three times. The second time He preceded the word "courageous" with a descriptive "very." Now why in the world would God repeat a call to courage to a stalwart, confident, and fearless hearer? I'd like to suggest God's man of the hour was quaking in his sandals.

The thirteenth chapter of Numbers records a rarely publicized fact about Joshua that I find very compelling. At the time of the first exploration of Canaan, he is listed in the census of leaders as "Hoshea son of Nun" (v. 8). A parenthetical portion of the sixteenth verse informs us that at some unspecified point "Moses gave Hoshea son of Nun the name Joshua." Scripture is clear that Moses knew Joshua would lead the conquest because God commanded him to lay hands on Joshua and commission him (Num. 27:18–20). We may not know when Joshua received his new name, but we don't have to be biblical scholars to reason why he might have needed one. In essence, the name Hoshea means deliverer while Joshua (Jehoshua) means *Jehovah* delivers. If I were flesh and blood chosen by God to lead a grasshopper people into a land of giant opposition, I'd want to know He was the true Deliverer, not me. I'd like to suggest that Joshua not only needed to know who he was, he needed to know who he wasn't. He wasn't God. Not a bad lesson for any of us to learn.

I love I am blessed, chosen, adopted, favored, redeemed, and forgiven.

So, what about us? Who does God say we are? If we've received Jesus as our personal Savior, the sum of our identity is found in 1 John 3:1: "How great is the love the Father has lavished on us, that we should be called the children of God! And that is what we are!" God spent no small amount of inspired ink expressing the various facets of sonship (and daughtership). Perhaps the most concentrated assessment of who we are in New Testament Scripture is found in Ephesians 1:3–8 (HCSB):

> Blessed be the God and Father of our Lord Jesus Christ, who has blessed us with every spiritual blessing in the heavens, in Christ; for He chose us in Him, before the foundation of the world, to be holy and blameless in His sight. In love He predestined us to be adopted through Jesus Christ for Himself, according to His favor and will, to the praise of His glorious grace that He favored us with in the Beloved. In Him we have redemption through His blood, the forgiveness of our trespasses, according to the riches of His grace that He lavished on us with all wisdom and understanding.

If we knew nothing else the New Testament had to say about us but accepted these few truths into our belief system, our lives would be altered. I ask you to consider memorizing these six descriptions so that when you say the third statement of our pledge of faith, you have at least an inkling of your worth. Because I'm a visual learner, pictures or diagrams often help me grasp a multifaceted concept as one whole. Take a look at the one below. (I decided to

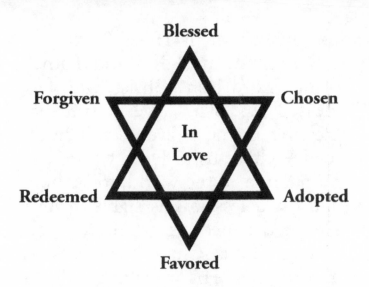

Blessed

Forgiven   Chosen

In
Love

Redeemed   Adopted

Favored

represent believers with a star because Philippians 2:15–16 says we "shine like stars in the universe" as we "hold out the word of life.")

At times the psalmist addressed his own soul as if to get through to his stubborn will (Ps. 42:5). How often you and I could use the same approach! Speak these words aloud to your own soul as many times as it takes to start believing it: In love I am blessed, chosen, adopted, favored, redeemed, and forgiven. Your soul is not the only one that needs to hear them. Keep these truths on the tip of your tongue so you can spit them at the accuser the next time you sense his condemnation (Rev. 12:10–11). The enemy knows that you and I will be too handicapped to live in consistent victory until we actively believe we are who, and what, God says we are.

Believing we are who God says we are has enormous results. Consider just a few:

A dramatically strengthened sense of security. Chosen, adopted, favored. What more could we need in order to feel secure? I love the phrase the KJV uses instead of "favored." We are "accepted in the beloved." If our stubborn minds would absorb that we are accepted by God because of Jesus Christ, our choices and subsequent behaviors would be profoundly affected. Think about the impact for a moment. What could be a bigger contributor to consistent defeat than insecurity? How many foolish decisions does it motivate? If you're like me, your insecurity propelled poor choices you didn't even want to make. I made some of my worst decisions in an attempt to be accepted. I was too insecure to go against the flow. I can't count the poor relational choices and the messes I made because of it. In our search for the root of our self-destructive tendencies, most of the time all we have to do is follow the stem of our insecurities. No matter how long we've been in bondage to it, we don't have to stay that way. The chains begin to break when we are willing to believe we are who God says we are.

Among numerous other casualties, our callings could be at stake if we don't allow God to deal with our chronic insecurities. When I was a little girl, I constantly hid behind my mother's skirt. I was first victimized as a very little girl. Though I was also loved and cared for by others, victimization of any kind undermines security. When the perpetrator is someone nearby who should have been trustworthy and protective, however, security virtually disintegrates. To make matters worse, I fell face-first into a table when I was six years old, and the result was the worst case of overbite in the free world. For several years prior to what seemed a lifetime of braces, I covered my mouth with my right hand when I was in public. Sometimes at the end of the day my shoulder throbbed. One insecurity birthed another until acceptance became my addiction. By adolescence I was a well-dressed, fairly poised, popular mess. And, boy, did I get messier.

God is the master of multitasking. According to Romans 8:30, all of us who are believers in Christ have a calling. I am convinced God assigns our callings for a host of reasons, many of which serve a purpose in us and not just those we'll serve. For example, God knew what He called me to do would force me to deal with the deeply embedded thorns of my past. I don't think God would be offended if I said He purposely picks on something until He can get it to surface. Of course, His motivation for surfacing the destructive parts of us is so we will face them and cooperate as He uproots them and heals our wounds. If God wanted to force me to face my insecurities head-on, He certainly chose an effective calling for me. Trust me on this: if you're insecure, you don't want to stand up in front of an audience and speak. Nor do you want to turn in a manuscript to editors. What I've been called to do exposes me constantly to criticism, constructive and otherwise. I am painfully aware of my weaknesses, flaws, and annoying habits. For crying out loud, I annoy myself! I have often said either God has a lot of grace or, frankly, He has poor taste.

God placed me in a position to have to wrestle with my fiercely handicapped identity and choose whom I'd believe: Him or me. Perhaps like some of you, I remake the decision almost every single day to believe I am who God says I am. The fact that I have not refused this public vocation or quit when the going got tough is a testimony to the pure tenacity of God to demand that I believe Him. I share this with you because I have a feeling some of you can relate. Has God also placed you in a position that seems to stir up every insecurity you have? Take it personally. He's stirring it up to scoop it out — often one spoonful at a time.

Anyone who assumes that those who are in leadership in the body of Christ are always confident and secure could hardly be more mistaken. Where they are worthy of a little respect is in their willingness to obey God's call over the screams of their own fears and insecurities. You must, too, if you want to fulfill your God-ordained destiny.

Righteousness credited to our account. Romans 4 frames one of my favorite revelations in all of Scripture. God knew people like me would need the New Testament update fiercely: "Abraham believed God, and it was credited to him as a gift" (v. 3). Obviously God thought the concept of faith credited as righteousness was pretty important, too, since He breathed it on the holy pages of Scripture numerous times. Take a look at Romans 4:1–5 and see the statement in context:

> What then shall we say that Abraham, our forefather, discovered in this matter? If, in fact, Abraham

was justified by works, he had something to boast about — but not before God. What does the Scripture say? "Abraham believed God, and it was credited to him as righteousness."

Now when a man works, his wages are not credited to him as a gift, but as an obligation. However, to the man who does not work but trusts God who justifies the wicked, his faith is credited as righteousness.

Beloved, absorb this principle: Every time we believe God, He credits it to our account as righteousness. The most obvious assumption would be that God credits righteous acts as righteousness, but the prophet Isaiah penned the disclaimer: "All of our righteous acts are like filthy rags" (Isa. 64:6). God insists in Scripture that believing Him is what He credits to our account as righteousness, and He gets to make the rules. As if to answer the skeptics who would try to deny the application to believers through the centuries, God removed all doubt in Romans 4:23, 25: "The words 'it was credited to him' were written not for him alone, but also for us to whom God will credit righteousness — for us who believe in him who raised Jesus our Lord from the dead."

Right about now those of you with a really good track record may be finding this concept a little hard to swallow. I know the feeling. I wrote part of this book while I was in Africa. After serving for a week at a missionary conference, I went with Keith on safari where I wrote while he hunted. (Four out of five of his trophies made the record books by the way. The kudu was most impressive.) We had a marvelous African chef who served us warthog ribs, wildebeast pie, and all sorts of other native delicacies. I savored every dish until the morning we had fried eggs and hippo. My children asked me how hippo tasted, and I told them to picture a hippo then imagine taking a bite out of it. That's exactly how it tasted. It had an uncanny way of getting fatter and fatter the more we chewed. I finally ended up spitting out what I was certain was a whole hippo into a napkin. Miss Manners could have been proud of me for not heaving at the dinner table.

To many, taking Romans 4:23–24 for exactly what it appears to say is too much to swallow. Some people fear that it could give license to sin, but we would be severely mistaken to rationalize God's grace and forgiveness into permission to act like pagans. Throughout this book I hope to prove to you biblically that those who presently and actively believe God are prompted to make wiser and much healthier decisions. Authentic faith cannot help but act. If we really believe God is who He says He is, that He can do what He says He can do, and that we are who God says we are, our decisions and our subsequent behaviors will reflect it. How we behave overwhelmingly flows from what we deeply believe. We'll see this principle illustrated further in the fourth point.

Freedom from the burden of our own sins. Take a fresh look at Romans 4:6–8:

> David says the same thing when he speaks of the blessedness of the man to whom God credits righteousness apart from works:
> "Blessed are they
> whose transgressions are forgiven,
> whose sins are covered.
> Blessed is the man
> whose sin the Lord will never count against him."

These verses must have meant as much to Paul with his sinful past as they mean to me. I suppose all of us who have histories of heinous sin cling to any affirmation that

God really can forgive and use those with terrible pasts. In Romans 4:8 God uses a powerful negation to extend our affirmation. In the Greek the word "never" is a double negative. In other words, we might read the passage like this: Blessed is the man whose sin the Lord will "no, never" count against him.

Relish the implication of God's choice to inspire the same Greek original for the word "credited" in Romans 4:3 ("credited to him as righteousness") and the word "count" in Romans 4:8 ("whose sin the Lord will never count against him"). Not surprisingly, it's an accounting term. Put the phrases side by side and something wonderful surfaces in the contrast. All that time I thought God was counting my sins, and He was counting my faith as righteousness instead.

Romans 1:17 says, "For in the gospel a righteousness . . . that is by faith from first to last, just as it is written: 'The righteous will live by faith.'" From first to last, faith is the heart of righteousness. Last year my oldest daughter, Amanda, called me on her cell phone to tell me she had just driven beside a car with a bumper sticker that read, "What if the hokeypokey is what it's all about?" I was preparing this lesson at the time. After a good laugh, the thought came to me that on the biblical subject of righteousness, faith is what it's all about. Stick that in your song and dance to it.

Don't misunderstand God covering our sins and not counting them against us to mean we can get away with anything. God is holy, and He will not be mocked. Furthermore, we'd learn little without chastisement and consequences for sin. The broad understanding based on the context of Romans is putting our faith in a God of grace who forgives the authentically repentant and henceforth "no, never" counts their sins against them. If these truths have the mercury in our self-righteousness meters rising, we may still be trying to take some credit for our acceptable standing before God through Christ. Grace is humbling, isn't it?

Obedience! Now some of us can relax. Hopefully this point will bring the concept of faith and righteousness into greater balance. A critical key dangles from the chain of Romans 1:5: "Through him and for his name's sake, we received grace and apostleship to call people from among all the Gentiles to the obedience that comes from faith." Take it in again: obedience comes from faith.

Beginning to believe I was who God said

I was had a profound influence on life between the ditches for me. For years I lived in a cycle of poor self-image followed by poor choices feeding a poorer self-image and even poorer choices. I became a Christian as a child, so don't bother trying to reason that my poor self-image was due to my unredeemed or ignorant state. Untrue. My continued poor self-image was directly due to believing my feelings and my past's prediction over my future rather than God's Word. In my latter twenties I began to study the Word of God in-depth. I had no idea at the time that God's first purpose for stirring an insatiable appetite for His Word was to perform intense and long-term surgery on my broken heart and distorted mind.

Through the study of His Word, I came upon Scripture after Scripture characterizing a child of God. Soon I began to believe them for others. Many of you who are Christian teachers or speakers may be able to relate to my unhesitant willingness to apply these characterizing Scriptures to anyone else but me. Surely someone besides me has confidently assured a hurting or questioning person of a biblical truth applying to her or him as a child of God that you didn't accept for yourself. Perhaps you've also noticed that God doesn't put up with that for very long. He has a strange penchant for consistency. God is adamant that we allow Him to teach to us what He wants to teach through us.

One way God hammered a biblical identity into my belief system was through a number of *this and that* conversations. Let me see if I can explain. When I saw Scriptures characterizing a child of God, I constantly sensed Him saying to my heart, "Beth, you are *this*." For a long time I still responded, "No, Lord, I am *that*." He and I both knew what I meant. Part of my *that* derived its names from the hurtful things others sometimes said behind my back. Your *that* may represent something entirely different, perhaps names you simply called yourself. Just think of a *that* as anything other than an Ephesians 1 *this*. Of course, God was right. I was *this*, but because I believed I was *that*, I still had a tendency to think and/or act like *that*. Months turned into years, and the voice of God grew increasingly insistent to my heart. "Beth, when will you ever believe you are *this?*" As my husband says, I am one hardheaded woman, but finally I began to respond, "OK, God.

I may be *this*, but my problem is that I still feel like *that*."

With a mustard seed of faith to at least

believe I was *this* even though I felt like *that*, God brought about a breakthrough. Through constant doses of His Word and a growing cooperation in my heart, He taught me to believe Him enough to at least start making decisions like a *this*. I would literally come to a crossroad of decision and think, "I still feel like *that*, but God says I'm *this*. How would a *this* behave in my current situation?" I'd even picture someone who I knew was a *this* and try to imagine what she'd do. Over and over I coached myself to make choices based on my *this* mentality. Not my old *that*. Over time my habits began to change, and I started behaving like *this*. After all, *this* is who I am.

All the while I was preoccupied with *this* and *that*, Romans 1:5 was hard at work. You see, my obedience flowed directly from my faith to believe I was who God said I was even when I didn't feel like it. Not surprisingly, the more I acted like *this* instead of *that*, the more I felt blessed, chosen, adopted, favored, redeemed, and forgiven. I guess that's why I'm like a dog gnawing on a bone in my unceasing insistence that anyone can live victoriously. Anyone can know the joy and fruit of obedience. Dear (equally hard-headed?) one, if I can live victoriously through the power of the Holy Spirit, anyone can.

We could think of many other examples of obedience coming from faith. For instance, sometimes we have to exercise faith to believe that obedience to God in a difficult situation will ultimately bear fruit even though it looks as though it might immediately cause hardship. We also have to exercise faith to believe God can handle the consequences of our obedience if someone important to us is not going to approve at first. For many of us, the step of faith begins much further back: we have to exercise faith to believe we are even capable of long-term obedience. And we are.

You see, God can relentlessly credit our faith as righteousness without concern that we'll take advantage of the freedom. He knows faith that does not lead to obedience is all talk and no walk.

I'd like to make a final observation on believing we are who God says we are in the context of Romans 4. Not coincidentally, this chapter of Scripture framing the concept of faith credited as righteousness specifies two Old Testament figures as examples: Abraham and David. They lived in very different eras and fulfilled different positions, yet they shared one commonality that related heavily to the concept of faith credited as righteousness. Both of them had sinned so grievously that their faith was demanded to believe they were still who God said they were: a father of multitudes and a king whose kingdom would never end. True restoration demands faith.

Peter could certainly attest to that.

"Simon, Simon, Satan has asked to sift you as wheat. But I have prayed for you, Simon, that your faith may not fail. And when you have turned back, strengthen your brothers" (Luke 22:31–32).

Why did Christ pray specifically for Simon Peter's faith not to fail? Peter's future was not dependent upon a perfect track record. It was dependent upon his faith. Peter would desperately need the courage to believe he was still who Christ said he was even after such failure. The result? The old fisher of men did indeed turn back and strengthen his brothers.

Peter believed God, and it was credited to him as righteousness.

Sometimes the hardest biblical truths to accept are about us. Believe you are who God says you are and fathom the double blessing of God crediting it to you as righteousness.

"Have I not commanded you? Be strong and courageous. Do not be terrified; do not be discouraged, for the LORD your God will be with you wherever you go."

Joshua 1:9

Chapter Eight

Believing You Can Do All Things Through Christ

You really can do it, you know. Whatever the harrowing path before you, you really can walk it victoriously. God will give you every place you step your feet for the glory of His name if you let Him. How do I know? For starters, Philippians 4:13 claims that a servant of God can do all things — *all* things — through Christ who gives him strength. That includes the otherwise impossible. Our fourth statement of faith isn't just a cheer. It isn't just a feel-good memory verse. It is sound theology yearning to become our reality.

I can do all things through Christ.

God will give you every place
you step your feet for the glory
of His name if you let Him.

I loved broadening our scope in our study of faith to include Moses, Abraham, and David in the last chapter. Each of their names made the team cut in the Hebrews 11 hall of faith. I was surprised and somehow refreshed to think that a measure of their challenge to walk by faith was likely found in continuing to believe they were who God said they were. I'd like to now set our sights back on Joshua, our primary protagonist, because he specializes in leading God's children to their promised lands of faith and fruitfulness. He was a man with a reputation for believing God against all odds. Though he lived centuries before Jesus, his example offers endless applications to New Testament believers. His example is going to help us understand and accept our fourth statement of faith. Through the might of the living God, Joshua did what he knew he could not do. Like us, he was told in advance he'd be able. We might call it preassurance rather than reassurance. Let's take a fresh look at that preassurance in Joshua 1:1–9.

After the death of Moses the servant of the LORD, the LORD said to Joshua son of Nun, Moses' aide: "Moses my servant is dead. Now then, you and all these people, get ready to cross the Jordan River into the land I am about to give to them — to the Israelites. I will give you every place where you set your foot, as I promised Moses. Your territory will extend from the desert to Lebanon, and from the great river, the Euphrates — all the Hittite country — to the Great Sea on the west. No one will be able to stand up against you all the days of your life. As I was with Moses, so I will be with you; I will never leave you nor forsake you.

"Be strong and courageous, because you will lead these people to inherit the land I swore to their forefathers to give them. Be strong and very courageous. Be careful to obey all the law my servant Moses gave you; do not turn from it to the right or to the left, that you may be successful wherever you go. Do not let this Book of the Law depart from your mouth; meditate on it day and night, so that you may be careful to do everything written in it. Then you will be prosperous and successful. Have I not commanded you? Be strong and courageous. Do not be terrified; do not be discouraged, for the LORD your God will be with you wherever you go."

In previous chapters we've talked about some of the differences between the old covenant and the new. We also celebrated the news in 2 Corinthians 3:10 that ours boasts a surpassing glory. I'd like to highlight another marvelous way the new exceeds the old. For perhaps a multitude of reasons, God seemed to speak and accomplish much of His work through one primary individual (or at the most a few) down through the ages in the Old Testament. Abraham, Isaac, Jacob, Joseph, Moses, Joshua, David, and an arm-long list of prophets pose a few examples. Certainly, God named twelve heads of the tribes of Israel, but Scripture doesn't suggest they were His spokesmen or specialized servants. As well, several prophets were contemporaries, but each one served his ordained sphere apart from the other. By and large, God seemed to accomplish His agenda most often through simple math: One plus one. I'd like to suggest that John the Baptist may have been the last prophet in the One plus one equation. As "a voice of one . . . in the desert" cried, "Prepare the way for the Lord" (Matt. 3:3), the fullness of the Godhead Himself came down from heaven to forever fulfill the one man calling to all humanity. He is Jesus "the One and Only, who came from the Father, full of grace and truth" (John 1:14).

No matter how mighty servants like Moses and Joshua were, "one and only" shoes tend to run large and slap around awkwardly on a walk. When Christ came to earth, He stepped His feet into those shoes, and, for the first time in all of history, they were a perfect fit. Wriggle your bare toes and celebrate that He's been wearing them ever since. No need to try them on. His plan henceforth was not to use just one but many: a corporate body of believers for each generation, each bringing his gifts to the mix. Christ broke the mold from the very beginning when He purposely commissioned twelve apostles.

Unlike the heads of the twelve tribes of Israel, Christ called His twelve to join Him in the very work He was doing. He commissioned them and supernaturally empowered them to accomplish divine tasks in His name. Further, Luke 10:1 tells us that "after this the Lord appointed seventy-two others and sent them two by two ahead of him to every town and place where he was about to go." They, too, were equipped and empowered to do in His name what they otherwise couldn't. Bug-eyed to be sure, they did "all things through Christ" who gave them strength (Phil. 4:13 KJV).

The New Testament math didn't stop with twelve plus seventy-two. In the Gospel of John, Christ gave the open invitation and basic requirement for accomplishing remarkable works in His name: "I tell you the truth, anyone who has faith in me will do what I have been doing. He will do even greater things than these, because I am going to the Father" (John 14:12). Anyone. That's a wide-open roster. Christ's final instructions before leaving planet Earth were, "Go and make disciples of all nations, baptizing them in the name of the Father and of the Son and of the Holy Spirit, and teaching them to obey everything I have commanded you. And surely I am with you always, to the very end of the age" (Matt. 28:19–20).

Let's get over the mentality that God mightily uses a few chosen people in each generation to fulfill His kingdom agenda and everyone else is basically insignificant. Under the inspiration of the Holy Spirit, Paul stressed the importance of the whole body of believers working together. Furthermore, he stated that "those parts of the body that seem to be weaker are indispensable, and the parts that we think are less honorable we treat with special honor . . . so that there should be no division in the body" (1 Cor. 12:22, 25). Christ left us too much to do to leave it up to a few. You are an honored part of the body of Christ, and your contributions add up. Remember, God's New Testament math specializes in addition and multiplication, not subtraction and division.

All you need to be mighty . . .
is a shield of faith and the sword of
the Spirit (the Word of God).
— Ephesians 6:16–17

This is a great time to repeat some of the concepts I stated in the first chapter of this book. You were meant to bring forth much fruit. You can be effective. Powerfully used. I'm talking to you. Not your preacher or Bible study teacher. Your legacy can still have an impact in a dozen generations if Christ tarries. You don't have to look a certain way, receive a certain gift, attend a certain denominational church, practice a certain kind of ministry, or establish a non-profit organization! All you need to be mighty in your generation is a shield of faith and the sword of the Spirit (the Word of God, Eph. 6:16–17). Through Christ you can absolutely, unequivocally do anything God places before you (Phil. 4:13). That includes getting the enemy off your Promised Land.

I had such fun raising two daughters near a dear friend raising her two sons. I remember when her oldest was in middle school and tried out for the football team. He was tall but so thin the football pads just made him look normal. His first game was against a team who obviously ate their Wheaties. The first time a large player ran toward him, he steeled himself for the hit, but in the split second before collision, a survival reflex seemed to take over. He stepped aside and motioned as if to say, "By all means, go right ahead." Don't think for a moment Satan is going to slow down when he sees you in the way. He has an arsenal of psychological weapons to keep your feet off promised ground. Prepare yourself in advance so you won't be caught off guard.

In Joshua 1:9 God warned Joshua not to

fall for two of the most effective deterrents to a Promised Land existence. "Do not be terrified; do not be discouraged."

Fear.

Discouragement.

In our previous chapter we touched on the element of fear in our discussion of insecurity. I'd like to explore it further at this time because fear is the very factor that keeps many of us from fleshing out our fourth statement of faith. We *can* do all things through Christ who strengthens us, but frankly we *won't* if we're too afraid to try. Satan will do anything he can to scare you away from your God-ordained destiny. I have wrestled with a stronghold of fear much of my life. Like you, my life challenges and long list of loved ones provide the enemy no few opportunities to prey on my fears. I have often heard the statistic that 90 percent of what we fear never comes to pass. Certainly, those statistics have proved true in my experience, but God has taught me as much from the 10 percent as the 90. Paradoxically, one of the ways God has cured many of my fears is to allow a few of them to come to fruition. After the crises came and went, He seemed to say to my heart, "Beth, did you live through it?"

"Well, yes, I guess I did."

"Was the devil able to use it to destroy you?"

"No, Sir. Apparently he wasn't."

"Are you still serving Me?"

"As a matter of fact, I am."

"Did you glean anything that might serve the body?"

"I believe I did. Volumes in fact."

"Do I still love you?"

"Undoubtedly, Lord."

"Do you still love Me?"

"More than ever, Lord."

"Why?"

"Because we made it. You and me."

Every now and then I ask those gathered in an audience how many have gotten through something shockingly well that they believed beforehand they couldn't bear. Hands never fail to raise all over the auditorium. Living through something we were sure we couldn't gives us a small glimpse of our inner man's immortality and clear evidence that Philippians 4:13 works for us too. None of us particularly like the face-it-until-you-get-over-it approach to fear banishment, but it can certainly be effective. Our insistence that "I could never survive if that happened to me" is not only an insult to the people who have already survived something similar.

It's an insult to a wonderful thing called grace. Where need abounds, grace more abounds. God's mercy is new every morning, and, like manna in the wilderness, He apportions it according to our need.

I listen to music constantly, so I often associate certain songs with certain seasons of my life. I recall going through a difficult time when a popular Christian song hit the radio waves with the following words: "You're not as strong as you think you are." One morning I insisted to God that I could not bear the circumstances that appeared inevitable in front of me. The song came back to my mind, only this time one word was different, as if God were making a point: "You're not as weak as you think you are." In fact, you can do all things through Christ who makes you strong. His power is made perfect in our weakness (2 Cor. 12:9).

Several years ago I wanted to go back to my favorite chain of mountains and stay in a cabin to write. Keith couldn't go at that time and asked me to take a friend with me to at least occupy a cabin nearby. I complied by asking a fellow Bible teacher from New York City who is as overstressed and overtired as I. Since Teresa had never been to that part of the country, I promised I'd take her to Yellowstone. The national park was only a few hours away from our cabin, and, among other things, I wanted her to see Old Faithful. I still find the geysers fascinating, and I knew she would too. We had been in the national park for some time when she looked anxiously ahead and said, "How much longer until we see Old Yeller?" Old *Yeller?* I laughed until I nearly ran off the road into a buffalo herd. Somehow the words Old Faithful and Yellowstone got a bit mixed up in her darling blonde head. Where I come from, *yeller* means cowardly. (If you have to say "yellow," don't bother.) Her faux pas made a perfect application for believing God. When all is said and done, you and I will either be Old Faithful or Old Yeller, but we won't be both. One will always elbow out the other.

God not only warned Joshua about fear, he also warned him about discouragement. "Do not be terrified; do not be discouraged." The word "discouraged" means all the things you might imagine, but I found there is one English synonym worthy of particular meditation: demoralization. As I reflected on the word *demoralization,* I felt like the Holy Spirit revealed an insight to me concerning one possible dimension of the word. I believe demoralization can occur when Satan figures out who you and I fear most that we are and what we fear we cannot do, then he sets out to confirm it. Can I get a testimony?

I could give you a dozen. Though I couldn't have articulated it, for years my deepest fear was that I was a weakling, powerless to temptation, and that I, the victim, would break under pressure every time. I was a victim, all right — a victim to my own erroneous belief system. Satan quickly detected my fears and preyed on them, doing everything he could to confirm what I believed. That's a powerful form of demoralization. Once again we see a huge reason we must believe we are who God says we are and we can do all things through Christ.

Immediately after God told Joshua not to be terrified or discouraged, He gave him the important reason. The reason had nothing to do with the absence of terrifying or discouraging circumstances. On the contrary, Joshua had never faced anything so frightful or potentially disparaging. What reason did God give Joshua for turning from fear and discouragement in the face of huge opposition? "The LORD your God will be with you wherever you go" (Josh. 1:9). When Jesus told His disciples not to be afraid in the storm, the reason wasn't the removal of their frightful circumstances but the presence of their Savior. "Take courage! It is I. Don't be afraid" (Matt. 14:27).

Remember, faith is never the denial of reality. It is belief in a greater reality. In other words, the truth may be that you are presently surrounded by terrifying or terribly discouraging circumstances. The reason you don't have to buckle to fear and discouragement is the presence of God in the middle of your circumstances. Call upon Him to step His One and Only shoes onto your territory and take over like the commander of the LORD's Army (Josh. 5:15). Hear Him say to you the words He said to Joshua: "Take off your sandals, for the place where you are standing is holy." That place, that circumstance, is holy because God stands on it with you. You don't have to fill His shoes, Dear One. Take off your sandals and walk barefoot in His wake.

A powerful preassurance God gave to Joshua is found in Joshua 1:5: "No man will be able to stand before you all the days of your life. Just as I have been with Moses, I will be with you; I will not fail you or forsake you" (NASB). In hopes that God will use this testimony to speak to you, I'd like to share how God seemed to place Joshua 1:5 like a road sign on my path several years ago.

One Saturday in the early fall I spoke at a conference with a great man of God. I had met him only briefly before, but we were scheduled to sit next to each other at a staff lunch just before I spoke. Knowing very little about me, he turned to me and casually said, "So, Beth, why do you limit God so much in your ministry?" I was stunned. I was also offended. The table went completely silent except for this same man who backed up his point with various pieces of evidence.

Though I tried to remain cool, my mind was swimming. I silently reasoned that he had to have talked to the chairman of my board. A few days earlier, my chairman and I had another round of frustrating conversation over the fact that, in matters involving Living Proof Ministries, I am what he affectionately calls a control freak. My chairman told me he felt God could have plans for further growth of the ministry that might eventually include some radio or even some television. I once again chanted my threefold mantra: I will never have a big staff. I will never do radio. And I certainly will never do television.

Defying my silent reasoning for his obvious gall, the out-spoken man at the conference and the chairman of my board had no connection at all, nor had he spoken with anyone else about the matter. He put me on the spot, asking me questions that surfaced all sorts of insecurities. Not the least of those questions was, "Can you admit God has given you a gift?" The question is enough to make anyone squirm, but add the grievous sins of my past to the mix, and all that remains is the unreasonable grace God showered to let me serve Him. I tend to want to apologize to other people in ministry for lowering the bar of leadership criteria. The man also had the nerve to ask if I might want to admit how often I criticize myself. No, I didn't want to "admit" anything. I just wanted to ask him if later he was going to be able to admit that a woman had given him a black eye. I finally turned to a staff member and quipped, "Are you going to let him continue this?" He grinned from ear to ear and said, "Absolutely! I'm enjoying every minute of it."

Perhaps this is a good time to interject that the man was never rude nor was his intention anything other than encouragement. Everyone at the table knew that but me. Lunch wasn't the end of the story. Right after I spoke, the church staff invited him back to the platform. When he dragged a single chair into the middle of the stage, I glanced at his associate and said, "If that's for me, I'm going to have to kill somebody." Of course it was. He invited the congregation to join him in praying for me because he was convinced God wanted to expand what He was doing in the ministry He had assigned to me. At the conclusion of the event, I was, in my family's words, fit to be tied.

Until that day I was never quite sure what my grandmother meant by a conniption. I had one on the way home all by myself in the car. "What was that?" I screamed toward heaven. I didn't get an answer, but I don't recall quieting enough to hear one. Over the next several days, my face reddened and my soul saddened over the many "nevers" I have said to God. When I finally started walking between the ditches, I adopted a set of spiritualized "nevers" to protect me from ever becoming like people in Christian media that I thought were weird. I now realize that at the heart of my list of "nevers" wasn't the desire to be like Christ. I don't doubt He can use media to further His kingdom. My desire was to not be like others. How arrogant can a person be in her attempt to be humble? The issue to God, however, was not growth of the ministry, participation in radio, or any other kind of media. The issue was authority. He is God, and He alone has the right to say what we will and will not do in our callings.

As I wept in prayer, I felt as if God spoke a gentle question to my heart: "Beth, what are you afraid of?" With bitter tears I blurted out, "I'm afraid I'll fail You!" Goodness knows I had before. I cried until I was sore. That next morning Kay Arthur was speaking in Houston, and I had the privilege of opening for her in prayer. I was absolutely desperate for a word from God, so I sat riveted on the front row. Not coincidentally, Kay's text that morning was Joshua chapter 1. At one point in her message, she walked down the platform stairs, looked straight at me, and passionately proclaimed a pointed phrase from Joshua 1:5. Using the New American Standard Bible (NASB) with classic Kay Arthur volume, she echoed God's words one at a time: "I–will–not–fail–you!"

From time to time someone will come

up to me after a conference and tell me she felt like she was the only one in the room as God seemed to speak straight to her. That day on the front row at Kay's conference, I knew the feeling. Only twenty-four hours earlier I bore my soul to God and confessed my worst fear: "I'm afraid I'll fail You!" Through His dear servant, God responded, "But, Beth, I will not fail *you*." I could still sob over it.

As resistant as I may have been, God also used His gutsy manservant to bring timely questions to the table the weekend earlier. He is a fine man God is using powerfully. We've since spoken several times and even laughed (a little) about it. He still declares he didn't have a clue that he had walked into the ring where Christ and I were wrestling. And just think how close he came to getting a black eye. Never let anyone tell you that ministry is the safe route.

Beloved, whether or not you want to admit it aloud, God has gifted you out of His glorious grace and for His name's sake. Christ has spoken over your life as His present-day disciple: "This is to my Father's glory, that you bear much fruit, showing yourselves to be my disciples." Perhaps, like me you have grievously failed God in the past. Perhaps, like me, your prior confidence was unknowingly in your own ability and determination to stay on track. I honestly thought my genuine love for Him would keep my handicapped feet on the path all by itself. I clearly remember telling God in my early twenties that no one would ever love Him more than I and that He'd never be sorry He called me. Then I fell headfirst into a pit. Tragically, not for the last time. Over and over the words rung in my head like church bells drowning in discord: I failed God! I failed God!

Somehow I don't think I'm the only one who ever felt that way. Failure takes all sorts of forms and hits all sorts of unsuspecting, sincere followers of Jesus Christ. We don't have to sin grievously to feel like we've failed. Sometimes all it takes is feeling like we've proved ineffective and untalented too many times to try again. What about you? Do you feel like you've failed God in some way? Are you too scared or discouraged to try serving God again? Have you allowed Satan to demoralize you by preying on your fear that you are nothing more than a failure? Then hear these words: God–will–not–fail–you! Grab onto Him with everything you have. Cast yourself entirely upon *His* ability to succeed and not yours. Blind yourself to all ambition except to please Him. Walk in the shadow of the Almighty. Grab onto the hem of His garment and find the healing and grace to go where He leads. In that place you will be equipped to do the impossible. There you can do all things through Christ who strengthens you.

Can you admit that God has gifted you? Can you admit how often you criticize yourself? Can you admit that some of your attempts at humility have been driven by pride? Can you admit that . . .

God is who He says He is?
God can do what He says He can do?
You are who God says you are?
You can do all thing through Christ?

I think I hear the familiar sound of a chair dragging across the floor to the center of the stage. This time it's not for me. It's for you. Humble yourself and sit down in it. Let Christ intercede for you according to the will of His Father. He knows the plans He has for you. Plans to give you a hope and a future. You can because He can.

"Do not let this Book of the Law depart from your mouth; meditate on it day and night, so that you may be careful to do everything written in it. Then you will be prosperous and successful."

Joshua 1:8

Chapter Nine

Believing God's Word
Is Alive and Powerful in You

You may find this hard to believe, but through the years I really have settled down a bit. The first ten years I spent in the Word, I believed that every doctrinal view I had been taught was absolutely right and that all other interpretations were unquestionably wrong, as were the people who held to them. Who in the world did I think I was? I was an aerobics teacher at our church gym, for crying out loud. I worked out all morning and studied Scripture all afternoon. I may have proved that nothing is more dangerous than a woman studying her Bible in her leotard, sweats, and leg warmers. I suppose I didn't do much harm. After all, who could have taken me seriously with my "heavy hands" and eighties hair? I've talked myself into becoming defensive. I'll have you know we were bright women in that class, even with side ponytails and purple leggings.

One way God widened my world was by pitching me out of the gym and into the heat of a spiritual war. He allowed the enemy to sift me like wheat, but only because I had some things that severely needed sifting. My personal world as I knew it fell apart in my early thirties. I had no idea at the time that God's plan was to heal me. For a while I was fairly certain the plan was to kill me. I didn't just break free. I was broken free. I spent the next several years in intensive care with God as He began rebuilding me from the inside out so I could teach harder lessons . . . but with a softer spirit.

An ongoing relationship with God through His Word is essential to the Christian's consistent victory!

While some rough edges have been softened through the years, some of those original convictions have only toughened. The priority of God's Word is undoubtedly one of them. I grow more convinced that an ongoing relationship with God through His Word is essential to the Christian's consistent victory. A few reasons why: We can't presently and actively believe God in our day-to-day challenges if we are not presently and actively in His Word. Romans 10:17 offers the most obvious link: "So then faith cometh by hearing, and hearing by the word of God" (KJV). God's direction for our lives will also escape us without the Word of God as "a lamp unto our feet and a light unto our path" (Ps. 119:105). Further, liberty in Christ becomes a reality in life through knowing and applying the truth of God's Word, not just taking our Bibles to church or keeping them on our nightstands. Psalm 119:11 also implies that hiding the Word in our hearts is a major safeguard against sin.

Ephesians 6:17 offers another vital reason the Word is essential to victory and one we'll repeat from time to time throughout this book: God's Word is our Sword of the Spirit, but we have to learn how to use it if we want to be a powerful force for the kingdom and against the darkness. Lastly, in terms of this book's central message, we'll never abide in our Promised Lands unless God's promises abide in us. God set the standard with Joshua when He told him to keep the Word continually on his tongue, meditate on it day and night, and live by its commands.

"Then you will be prosperous and successful" (Josh. 1:8). With all my heart I believe living on and by God's Word is still the key to true success.

Recently my husband (and sometimes resident cynic), Keith, asked me why all of the sudden everyone at church seems to be talking about having a "life verse." I shrugged and explained that certain buzzwords and phrases seem to come and go in church culture. I told him that a "life verse" appears to be a Scripture a believer feels most captures his or her testimony or relationship with God. He asked me what I thought mine was, and I quipped, "Repent, lest ye die." (After my past history of sin, God and I have an agreement. If any fruit comes from my life, I give Him all the glory, and He lets me live.) After Keith and I shared a good belly laugh, I gave the question some thought.

God's Word is our Sword of the Spirit, but we have to learn how to use it if we want to be a powerful force for the kingdom and against the darkness.

I seem to have a new favorite verse every day, but Living Proof Ministries derived its name and purpose from Hebrews 4:12, a

Scripture God used to steer an entirely new direction for my life. The Amplified Bible expresses it best: "For the Word that God speaks is alive and full of power [making it active, operative, energizing, and effective]; it is sharper than any two-edged sword, penetrating to the dividing line of the breath of life (soul) and [the immortal] spirit, and of joints and marrow [of the deepest parts of our nature], exposing and sifting and analyzing and judging the very thoughts and purposes of the heart."

Alive, active, operative, energizing, effective. Pretty impressive elements, don't you think?

Don't miss the crucial tie between the Word of God and the people of God in this verse. God not only told us that His Word is alive, effective, and powerful on its own — He insisted that it is alive, effective, and powerful in us when we receive it. Pause and let that truth sink in. I'm convinced most of us don't begin to appreciate and assimilate this revolutionary precept. Unlike any other text, the Word of God has supernatural effects for those who receive it by faith. When we receive it by reading it, meditating on it, believing it, and applying it, the life of the Word becomes lively in us. The power of God's Word becomes powerful in us. The activity of the Word becomes active in us. The operations of the Word become operative in us. The energy of the Word becomes energizing in us. The effectiveness of the Word becomes effective in us. In fact, according to Hebrews 4:12, when we receive God's Word, it invades every part of our being, even the marrow of our bones and the motives of our hearts.

God doesn't speak just to hear the sound of His own voice. Interestingly, neither does He speak to be heard by others. He speaks in order to accomplish. This aim proves consistent from the beginning of time. Genesis 1:3 records the first words out of His mouth where humankind is concerned: "And God said, 'Let there be light,' and there was light." Isaiah 55:10–11 expresses the intention of His Word:

> As the rain and the snow
> come down from heaven,
> and do not return to it
> without watering the earth
> and making it bud and flourish,
> so that it yields seed for the sower
>   and bread for the eater,
> so is my word that goes out from
>   my mouth:

It will not return to me empty,
but will accomplish what I desire
and achieve the purpose for which I
sent it.

God's Word possesses accomplishing power and achieving power. That's a fact. But I want it to have accomplishing and achieving power in me. Thankfully, so does God. One of the most prominent changes in my approach to God is that I've become very intentional about thanking Him for the quickening power of His Word in me, claiming and believing that He is energizing it to accomplish and achieve His desires, even at the very moment I receive it. As I sit before God on my back porch every morning and place that day's schedule and petitions before Him in prayer, I receive my daily Bible reading like an athlete might eat an energy bar. I often read that day's portion of the Word aloud and actively participate in receiving it into my belief system. (I do this by taking a moment to meditate on it. I might ask myself questions like: "Do I really believe these words? And, if I do, how does it show? Are there ways I might be able to act on the truth of these words today? How do these words apply to my present challenges and petitions today?" I also ask Him to take those words and sow them deep into my otherwise deceptive heart and even into my subconscious mind.) I count on those Scriptures in my morning Bible reading to become active, energizing, and powerful in me that day.

And they do.

Because that's what they were meant to do.

I have loved God's Word for a long time, but my approach and expectation have changed dramatically as my confidence in Him has grown. In the old days I used to expect a little direction and the increase of a little knowledge from my daily Bible reading; therefore, those were the dividends I was most often aware of receiving. Now I add to those expectations liveliness, energy, and empowerment from the Word, counting on its effectiveness in advance. As I go through my day meeting inevitable challenges and self-doubts, I will often think or say aloud, "Lord, Your Word is alive and active in me today, and I thank You for its achieving and accomplishing power. Make it effective in me today and make me effective in You today."

That's not all I ask. I also know what healing God has brought to me through His Word, so I actively pray verses like

Psalm 107:20 and Proverbs 4:20–22 over my life and my loved ones' lives.

Psalm 107:20 says, "He sent forth his word and healed them."

Proverbs 4:20–22 says, "My son, pay attention to what I say; listen closely to my words. Do not let them out of your sight, keep them within your heart; for they are life to those who find them and health to a man's whole body."

When I study God's Word, I often ask that He'll make me a healthier person in any way He sees fit as a direct result. I know that my Amanda, Curt, and Melissa also seek God through His Word every day, so I ask the same thing for them and my husband, Keith. Likewise, I ask God to send forth His healing words to those who participate in the Bible studies He's given me. I will joyfully receive any application of that precept He desires, whether it is a work toward spiritual, emotional, mental, or physical wholeness. I continually count on God's Word accomplishing greater wholeness in every true hearer no matter what form it takes. Forget legalism! However God cares to apply the power and effectiveness of His Word to my life and my loved ones, I want us to receive it!

If your expectation of God's Word in

your life has been small, I am asking you to consider giving it far more credit. Second Timothy 3:16 says, "All Scripture is God breathed," so don't just read it like any other inspirational or instructional text. Inhale it! Jeremiah 15:16 says, "Your words came, I ate them; they were my joy and my heart's delight, for I bear your name, O LORD God Almighty." Try Jeremiah's approach while you're at it. Don't just read God's Words. Receive them like a famished man at a feast. Whether we imagine inhaling it or devouring it, "let the word of Christ dwell in [us] richly" (Col. 3:16). Ask God to cause it to abide in you and bring its properties of effervescent life, power, and effectiveness with it. How about something moving into your life with some positive baggage for a change? Believe God to accomplish and achieve something eternal and intentional through your Scripture meditation every single day. Grow in confidence that every word abiding in you is having powerful effects.

The primary reason God's Word can have such an effect on a believer's daily life is its vital association with the Holy Spirit.

The primary reason God's Word can have such an effect on a believer's daily life is its vital association with the Holy Spirit. When we receive Christ as our Savior, the actual Spirit of Christ or the One we call the Holy Spirit takes up residency in us. First Corinthians 6:19 refers to us as temples of the Holy Spirit. This Holy Spirit living within us has a very strong connection to the Word of God that can easily be viewed in John 14:17 and 2 Timothy 2:15. The former calls the Holy Spirit the "Spirit of truth," while the latter calls Scripture the "word of truth." In the same way that sin quenches the Holy Spirit within us, Scripture quickens the Holy Spirit within us. In fact, when we are filled with the Holy Spirit by yielding to His Lordship and we read and receive God's Word, something virtually supernatural takes place. You might think of it as internal combustion. Let me explain:

In Jeremiah 23:29, God said, "Is not my word like fire . . . ?" As we draw from this parallel, relating something we can't quite understand to something we can, picture the Holy Spirit like a flammable substance within us. Because oil was often associated with anointing in the Word, many scholars believe oil symbolized the Holy Spirit. For the sake of our analogy, let's imagine the Holy Spirit as flammable oil within us. Now, imagine this oil flooding us completely as we seek and receive by faith the filling of God's Holy Spirit. Next, imagine taking the torch of God's Word and combining it with the oil of the Holy Spirit. What is the result? The consuming fire of our God blazes within us, bringing supernatural energy, glorious activity, and pure, unadulterated power. If you like formulas, this is one I believe you can count on:

> The Spirit of truth + the Word of truth = internal combustion

Sometimes I actually feel the Holy Spirit within me quickening to the Word of God as I study it, mix it with faith, and pray to absorb it. Even when I don't feel a thing, I count on super-natural fireworks within. God says His Word is alive and powerful, and I believe Him. He also says His Word is alive and powerful when it's in me.

Me: a bundle of faults, fears, and insecurities.

Just think! My weakness is not strong enough to wound God's Word. Neither is yours. God does His job. He speaks to accomplish. We don't have to make Him. We just need to let Him.

Finally! We get to add our fifth statement to our pledge of faith. Write the other four and spend a moment with God celebrating the fifth:

- _____
- _____
- _____
- _____

God's Word is alive and active in me.

Believe it and receive it.

"I believe;
therefore I have spoken."

2 Corinthians 4:13

Chapter Ten

Believing God to Put His Word on Your Tongue

Our previous chapter centered on the life and power of the Word. We learned an important principle: God not only speaks to be heard; God also speaks to accomplish. His words have accomplishing and achieving power; and when we receive them by faith and through obedience, they have accomplishing and achieving power in us.

Mankind possesses complete uniqueness among all creatures because we were created in the image of God. Our unique ability to communicate through words is one of the most obvious evidences of the image we bear. The element of divine communication transmitted to the inhabitants of earth is so critical, so paramount, that Christ is called the Word that "became flesh, and dwelt among us" (John 1:14 NASB). By virtue of our creation in our divine Communicator's image, I'd like to suggest that our words possess an element of accomplishing and achieving power too. Proverbs 18:21 says, "The tongue has the power of life and death." With the exception of kings, judges, and dictators, the application is primarily figurative; but, make no mistake, it is far from diminutive. We possess no small power in our tongues. Most of us can testify that the human tongue owns the power to kill all sorts of things. Relationships, lifelong dreams, and self-confidence are only a few of the common fatalities. Thankfully, perhaps as many of us have also experienced life-giving words of encouragement, instruction, and exhortation.

God's words are omnipotent.
Our words are potent.

Recently my praise team and I were sharing a meal at a Houston restaurant after a simulcast, and I glanced over at an adjacent table only to see my high school English teacher. I was blessed enough to study under her graciously demanding teaching both my junior and senior year. I lost touch with her after graduation but have for years wanted to come face-to-face with her to express my gratitude. She was the first person who ever suggested that I had a writer buried somewhere within me. I fell into much sin, hypocrisy, and despair after those days and was certain that whatever promise I may have possessed at one time, I forfeited by my foolishness. God is so merciful, and He makes His promises good for His own name's sake. He used that high school English teacher many times through the years when I was flooded with self-doubt. After many books and Bible studies, I still don't see myself as a writer, but every now I then I think, *Mrs. Fanett did.* Never underestimate the power of words. You no doubt have your own stories. And what an interesting thought that others have their stories about the impact of our words. I wonder what they'd say?

Words wield power, both divine and mortal.

We might think of the comparison of the power of words like this:

God's words are *omnipotent.* Our words are *potent.*

God's words possess omnipotent achieving and accomplishing power. Our words can have potent achieving and accomplishing power.

A vital element in learning to walk by

faith and obedience is learning to *talk* by faith and obedience. Both the Bible and personal experience teach us that human words possess much power. In fact, James 3:4 compares the tongue to the small rudder with the power to steer a large ship. James 3:6 compares the tongue to a fire that can corrupt and set aflame the whole person. Our words are potent no matter how we use them, but what would happen if we allowed God to take hold of them?

I'd like to suggest to you that we have no greater built-in vessel for the external expression of divine power than our mouths. Perhaps that's why Satan will do anything he can to set the tongue aflame with the fire of hell (James 3:6). He knows who holds the tongue can often hold the whole man. The tongues of God's people are meant to be set ablaze by the holy fire of heaven, accomplishing and achieving that which glorifies God. James 3:2 suggests that a chief sign of Christian maturity is a tamed tongue. Of this I'm certain: a sanctified mouth is too unnatural to ever be coincidental. If we want it, we're going to have to pursue it regularly and cooperate with God to receive it.

One primary way God sanctifies our tongues is to put His Word on it. The first strategy God gave Joshua for living victoriously and successfully in the Promised Land holds great significance. Before God told Joshua to meditate on His Word and live by its precepts, He issued this command: "Do not let this Book of the Law depart from your mouth" (Josh. 1:8). What did God mean? Keep My Word on the tip of your tongue!

In the Old Testament the practice of meditation did not involve the thought life alone. It involved the mouth. In fact, some of the English meanings of the Hebrew word for *meditation* are "to murmur, mutter, speak, whisper." One definition adds that meditation "denotes a variety of utterances."[4] To the ancient Hebrew mind, a vital part of meditation was repeating a precept or a particular phrase of Scripture with the tongue and actually talking it over, even with oneself, while reflecting and thinking on it.

At this moment on our journey to the Promised Land, we are stumbling onto something of great importance. In my opinion, the precept we're about to consider is in many ways where the rubber on our hiking boots meets the road. What you do with this chapter may well determine whether you will simply read another

Christian book, albeit encouraging, or become armed and dangerous to the kingdom of darkness in the fight of faith.

One primary way God sanctifies our tongues is to put His Word on it.

I have shared before that my husband is the epitome (even caricature) of what many picture a Texas man to be. Although he wouldn't be caught dead wearing a big belt buckle, he wears a cowboy hat, Wranglers, and one pair or another of a wide assortment of cowboy boots in his closet. He doesn't just wear the part; he acts the part. He is a dyed-in-the-wool Texas trophy hunter. I, a pacifist by nature, do not share his tastes in hobbies. I prefer books to kills, explaining why we call ourselves Keith the barbarian and Beth the librarian. I do, however, love the simplicity and relaxation of the life that surrounds his Texas sports.

Last spring I grabbed a Christian novel and went with Keith to the deer lease to close camp for the year. Late one afternoon we went for a walk with our two dogs. I balked when Keith grabbed a shotgun, but he was quick to remind me of numerous wild hogs and snakes in the vicinity, posing as much a threat to us as the dogs. As usual, he walked with the shotgun broken open and disengaged over his right forearm, safely separating the barrels from the trigger mechanism and handle. In his other hand was the leash attached to our fine bird dog. I had our other trusty dog (my best friend for ten years) on the other leash.

In the wilderness of temptation,
Christ set an example of responding
with the Word of God
when under satanic assault.

About a mile into our walk, my dog, Sunny, lunged suddenly and fiercely at something in front of her. My eyes didn't have time to adjust to the object of her fury before Keith had snapped the gun back into one piece, pitched it up so he could catch it by the trigger, and blew a rattler's head to bits. All with one arm. I'm talking *Gunsmoke* here. All we lacked was a swoon and a sweep. I was so impressed I nearly dropped to the ground. I couldn't get a single word out of my mouth. All I could do was look wide-eyed at my husband in astonishment and think, *What a man!*

We're going to see that having God's

Word ready on the tip of our tongues has numerous advantages, but Keith illustrated far from the least of them. Having God's Word on the tip of our tongues is like having a loaded shotgun on our walks to and through our Promised Lands. As long as we're armed, we can walk leisurely and peacefully because at a moment's threat, we are loaded and ready to shoot the head off that "ancient serpent called the devil" (Rev. 12:9). Think of the head representing authority. A stronghold is any way the devil tries to presume authority in our lives. If we belong to Christ, Satan has no right to exercise authority over us, but he hopes we're too ignorant regarding Scripture to know it. In the wilderness of temptation, Christ set an example of responding with the Word of God when under satanic assault. Knowing and claiming God's Word when attacked blows the head off enemy forces.

We don't have to be faced with a demonic enemy to need the Word of God ready on our tongues. We only need to be faced with our own weaknesses, doubts, day-to-day challenges, and other sojourners with the same. Second Corinthians 4:7–13 describes living powerfully amid undeniable trials. It concludes with a potent directive we can associate with Joshua 1:8 and the Word on our tongues:

> But we have this treasure in jars of clay to show that this all-surpassing power is from God and not from us. We are hard pressed on every side, but not crushed; perplexed, but not in despair; persecuted, but not abandoned; struck down, but not destroyed. We always carry around in our body the death of Jesus, so that the life of Jesus may also be revealed in our body. For we who are alive are always being given over to death for Jesus' sake, so that his life may be revealed in our mortal body. So then, death is at work in us, but life is at work in you.
>
> It is written: "I believed; therefore I have spoken." With that same spirit of faith we also believe and therefore speak.

Take a moment to practice a little Hebrew meditation regarding that last sentence.

"With that same spirit of faith we also believe and therefore speak."

Certainly the word "spirit" in 2 Corinthians 4:13 refers to the essence or idea of immaterial life as it does elsewhere, but the most literal meaning of the Greek word *pnuema* is "breath." For the sake of application, if we momentarily replace the word spirit with the word *breath,* the verse reads, "With that same breath of faith we also believe and therefore speak."

Remember, "all Scripture is God-breathed" (2 Tim. 3:16), so in regard to God's Word, picture this practice like receiving spiritual CPR. We can read Scripture for hours, but if we don't receive it by faith, it doesn't abide in us, bringing its vitality, energy, and effectiveness. We may be encouraged, but we are neither empowered nor changed. If we do receive it by faith — thereby accepting it into our belief system — we might think of the practice like inhaling a breath of faith. Then, when we choose to speak what we believe, we might think of ourselves as exhaling that same breath into speech. Of course, neither the Word nor the Spirit of God ever departs. Rather, they impart. Let's take a look at the process step-by-step:

1. We read or hear God's Word.
2. We choose to receive it, thereby inhaling it like a fresh breath of faith.
3. We speak it aloud at opportune times, even just to ourselves, thereby

exhaling that spirit of faith over our very circumstances.

Making a reasonable and livable lifestyle of believing and speaking God's Word is like living on the CPR of the Holy Spirit. Don't try to make something mystical out of it. Nothing is more practical. The idea is that the more we believe the Word and then take the opportunity to speak that same Word, concept, or application, the more we actively live and breathe faith. This practice can take place through . . .

- reading Scripture aloud.
- memorizing Scripture.
- meditating on Scripture.
- seizing opportunities to discuss scriptural truths in a class, with a friend, or with family.
- doing likewise with scriptural concepts or applications.

Mind you, I'm not suggesting berating people with Scripture. In terms of our analogy, we might call that bad breath. A fresh word comes out of our mouths with fresh breath.

Remember our formula in the last chapter?

The Spirit of truth + the Word of truth = internal combustion

How does inhaling (through believing) and exhaling (through speaking) a fresh breath of faith fit in? "Believing and therefore speaking" is one way we externalize the internal passion. We take the passion and life of what is happening within us and externalize it through speech. Speech, by the way, that is not just for the sake of being heard but for the ultimate purpose of accomplishing and achieving in the image of its Creator. Encouragement, instruction, exhortation, counsel, and, yes, even at times the issue of an appropriate rebuke are a few ways God's Word upon our tongues can accomplish and achieve. God's Word upon our tongues certainly doesn't always externalize through exact Scripture recitation. It often takes the form of simple godly conversation. Isaiah 50:4 offers a wonderful example of our precept: "The Sovereign LORD has given me an instructed tongue, to know the word that sustains the weary. He wakens me morning by morning, wakens my ear to listen like one being taught."

Oh, the positive power of an instructed tongue! How many weary people do we encounter day after day who could use a sustaining word?

You may wonder, "Aren't actions more

powerful than words?" Without a doubt we externalize the internal works of the Spirit through action as well. Speech without action is talk without walk. In this chapter, however, I'm talking about a different practice and purpose: the specific power that is released when we "believe and therefore speak." If you've fully participated in the faith practices I proposed to you early in our journey, you've actually practiced a perfect example of "believing and therefore speaking." Every single time you say your five-statement pledge of faith, you are speaking what you believe.

You may ask, "Do we always have to say them out loud? Can't we simply think the words?" Absolutely! But have you noticed that the statements seem to take on an added element of power when you say them aloud? That's no coincidence. Created in the image of our omnipotent God, our spoken words are potent. If you'll pardon the comparison, speaking what we believe — like our five-statement pledge of faith — is like inviting our souls to a pep rally. Somehow, vocalized words can stir more enthusiasm even from when ourselves to ourselves.

We can't talk about the God-endorsed power of words without specifying prayer.

Every time we make a petition to God, we are using words that have elements of accomplishing and achieving power, even if we pray silently. God hears the words and communications of our minds as clearly as human ears hear our spoken words.

"O LORD, . . . you perceive my thoughts from afar. . . . Before a word is on my tongue you know it completely, O LORD" (Ps. 139:1–2, 4).

I have found, however, that I sense more power in prayer when I "believe and therefore speak" out loud. Please understand, the difference rests in me rather than God. He hears and receives petitions of any kind that are prayed in Jesus' name. Praying aloud and vocally assuming my right of sonship (daughtership, of course) somehow builds my faith and confidence in God and the practice of prayer. I don't know about you, but I tend to be a lot gutsier in my vocalized prayers because hearing them with my own ears often ignites my heart and mind all the more.

Not long after God called me to this revival of faith, I read John 15:7 with a new outlook, and I was startled by the revelation. If it's familiar to you, read it as if you've never heard it before: "If you remain in me and my words remain in you, ask whatever you wish, and it will be given you."

I have a news flash for anyone who doesn't know it: We're supposed to be experiencing lots of answered prayer. I said lots of it. John 15:7 is an important part of Christian theology that is meant to be a Christian reality. I have a feeling much of the body of Christ feels like I did for so long. On a scale of one to ten based on the sense of God's presence and apparent response, I could have rated my prayer life a pitiful two. Don't misunderstand me, I prayed all the usual "bless and protect us" prayers, but my ordinary mode of operation was to pray things that looked like they were probably going to turn out anyway. Can anyone relate? Then God began calling me out of my unbelief.

My prayer life changed and matured gradually through the years as I sought God through His Word, but something dramatic happened that suddenly pitched it forward. I hate to admit it, but it came out of a sense in prayer one day that, frankly, God was bored with my prayer life. As I explained in *Praying God's Word*, I sensed God saying, "My child, you believe Me for so little. Don't be so safe in the things you pray. Who are you trying to keep from looking foolish? Me or you?"[5] You see, sometimes I decided that I'd rather not ask certain things than risk a no. I reasoned that God was sovereign and I'd simply let Him do what He wanted. In reality, I was terrified that God or I would let me down and shake what little faith I had. The question I believe I heard from the Holy Spirit still convicts and chills me. That was the official Day One of my personal faith revival.

According to John 15:7, the key to answered prayer is sharing the mind of Christ over any given matter through His words actively abiding in us. The more His words roll around in our heads, the more likely we are to think with them. I doubt many believers ever grow to the point that they know the mind of Christ well enough to continually pray petitions He answers affirmatively. We can, however, mature in our prayer life enough to see far more affirmative answers than we have.

The key to answered prayer
is sharing the mind of Christ
over any given matter through
His words actively abiding in us.

One of the most evidentially powerful

ways I "believe and therefore speak" in prayer is by using Scripture. I often speak and apply Scripture when I vocalize my most serious requests. At these times I may sense a double portion of power and confidence, and for good reason. As I explained in *Praying God's Word*, combining prayer and Scripture is like tying together two sticks of dynamite. I've found no more powerful tool especially for warfare prayer and praying down strongholds. I also might use Scripture over matters that require long periods of time, such as the salvation of a resistant sibling. I often interject Scripture into requests for miraculous intervention as well. Each scenario I've named represents a time most tempting to dwindle in faith, energy, and longevity in prayer. When I use Scripture, I in effect transfer the burden to God's Word rather than my ability to pray correctly or adequately. Remember: Because it comes from God's own divine mouth, His Word has energy and power all its own. I let it do the work.

Let's look at one more example of "believing and therefore speaking" before we conclude this chapter. Do you remember when Christ told His disciples that if they had faith as small as a mustard seed, they could say to a mountain, "Move from here to there" and it would move? The next words out of Christ's mouth were "Nothing will be impossible for you" (Matt. 17:20). Christ did not tell His disciples only to "think" with faith-filled authority, nor did He tell them to perform certain physical demonstrations. He distinctively told them to have faith and "say to this mountain." In other words, I think we could say that Christ taught His disciples to "believe and therefore speak."

I think we, too, could speak to some mountains at appropriate times and they just might move. In case that makes you nervous, let me assure you that I, too, have seen the misuse and abuse of concepts like this through practices that involve disturbing shouts and rebukes (as if the louder the better) and presumptuous naming and claiming. My plea is that we not miss the use because of misuse. The concept of God assigning or entrusting limited authority, under the umbrella of His own, to His children is consistent from Genesis to Revelation. Instead of playing it safe, we could go to the trouble to learn and exercise the proper use of biblical authority. If we are uneducated, easily intimidated, or turned off, all Satan has to do is fan the flame of misuse in various pockets of the body of Christ and the rest will forfeit the appropriate exercise. Satan has much to gain by turning us off to faith practices.

We walk in faith when He invites us based on a working knowledge of His Word and a balanced prayer life.

"Believing and therefore speaking" is an example of exercising a dimension of biblical authority under the rule and Word of God alone. If we truly believe according to the sound application of Scripture that God is extending authority to us as His children over a certain matter, we might be shocked what we could tell to "Move!" and it would. I've tried telling a few mountains to move at times (mostly in private) and, low and behold, to this Baptist girl's surprise, some have! These "mountains" can take any number of forms. Sometimes I might in effect speak to a ridiculous, time-consuming conflict to be resolved. Other times a huge obstacle suddenly arises in my path or the path of my loved one, and I just might have courage enough to tell it to move. I've been under the threat of countless delays that could have kept me from fulfilling an obligation, and occasionally I might speak to it like a mountain and tell it to get out of my way. Living in Houston, I've had numerous opportunities to tell some traffic to move, and every now and then I feel like the Red Sea has parted in front of me. I've had some fun learning to exercise my weak and awkward faith and see it grow a bit. I don't mind telling you that I think He's gotten a kick out of it too. I don't doubt He's laughed out loud at some of my attempts to say to some mountains, "Move!"

By any stretch of the imagination am I suggesting we always tell our obstacles to move rather than ask our heavenly Father to move them? By no means! First of all, any supernatural results of biblical practices come from God alone. If a mountain moves, God moved it. He simply invited us to join Him by allowing us to exhale a powerful breath of the Spirit. Having the faith to tell a mountain to move and asking God to move the mountain are not opposing concepts. Like many biblical practices, we don't replace one with the other. We seek to be led by the Holy Spirit and discern when to implement certain practices. God alone must be the initiator in matters of faith (Heb. 12:2). We walk in faith where He invites us based on a working knowledge of His Word and a balanced prayer life. The same Jesus who told His disciples that they could "say to this mountain, 'Move from here to there,' " also taught them to ask for what they needed or wished in prayer (John 15:7). The common denominator is that both practices are ways we "believe and therefore speak."

I want you to seek God for yourself on this matter and all others I set before you, but I'll share with you how I usually handle a mountain. If I am walking with God and seeking to be filled by His Spirit, I usually act upon what Romans 12:3 calls "the measure of faith God has given [me]" in whatever situation arises. By a long shot, most of the time when faced with a mountain, my present and active faith prompts me to pray believing prayers. I might say, "Lord, I believe You have called me to do a particular thing or reach a particular person, but an obstacle has risen in my way. Since I believe Your will is for me to accomplish something on the other side of that mountain, I believe You to move it, in Jesus' name. Amen." Other times and for reasons I can't always explain, I am just suddenly filled with the faith in God and the filling of the Spirit to say, "Move!" to that mountain. And it often does. I'm grinning with pleasure in God as I think about it.

Would you be offended if I told you that I not only think God is awesome, wonderful, and faithful but that I also think He is fun? In fact, in my opinion those who take the faith out of spiritual living have taken the fun out of life. They can play it safe and hug the tree trunk if they want, but I like living out on a limb with God. I've put all my hopes and all my faith in Him. I have absolutely nothing else to hang on to. I'm banking on God and His Word with every breath and every drop of energy I have. If He doesn't come through, I've made a fool of myself. But I'm not worried, because He has yet to fail me. No, I've not always gotten what I've asked, nor has every mountain moved. I'll show you what I've learned to assume when a mountain won't budge. My basis is the context of the original directive in Matthew 17.

In verse 20 Jesus said, "If you have faith as small as a mustard seed, you can say to this mountain, 'Move from here to there' and it will move. Nothing will be impossible for you." Notice that Christ didn't generalize His illustration with "any" mountain. He specifically said "this" mountain. To what mountain did He refer? If you'll check the context, Jesus and three of His disciples had just come down from the mountain where He was transfigured before them.

When Jesus specifically said, "You can say to *this* mountain" (author's emphasis), I believe He pointed to the same mountain.

So there you have it. Beloved, if you pray that God will move a mountain and He doesn't, or you have the faith to tell a mountain to move and it won't, assume Christ wants you to climb it instead and see Him transfigured. Either way the mountain is under your feet.

"The one who trusts in him will never be put to shame" (Rom. 9:33).

"With the tongue we praise our Lord and Father, and with it we curse men, who have been made in God's likeness. Out of the same mouth come praise and cursing. My brothers, this should not be."

James 3:9–10

Chapter Eleven

Believing God
Can Sanctify Your Mouth

A vital part of learning the walk of faith in our journey to and through the Promised Land is learning the talk of faith. A glimpse at the book of Numbers offers all the evidence we need to view the impact of faithless talk on our way to our Canaans. The following account records the return of the Israelite spies who were sent ahead to explore the land God had promised His people:

> They came back to Moses and Aaron and the whole Israelite community at Kadesh in the Desert of Paran. There they reported to them and to the whole assembly and showed them the fruit of the land. They gave Moses this account: "We went into the land to which you sent us, and it does flow with milk and honey! Here is its fruit. But the

people who live there are powerful, and the cities are fortified and very large. We even saw descendants of Anak there. The Amalekites live in the Negev; the Hittites, Jebusites and Amorites live in the hill country; and the Canaanites live near the sea and along the Jordan."

Then Caleb silenced the people before Moses and said, "We should go up and take possession of the land, for we can certainly do it." [Sounds like statement 4 to me!]

But the men who had gone up with him said, "We can't attack those people; they are stronger than we are." And they spread among the Israelites a bad report about the land they had explored. They said, "The land we explored devours those living in it. All the people we saw there are of great size. . . . We seemed like grasshoppers in our own eyes, and we looked the same to them." [Sounds like they needed to recite statement 3.]

That night all the people of the community raised their voices and wept aloud. All the Israelites grumbled against Moses and Aaron, and the whole assembly said to them, "If only we had died in Egypt! Or in this desert! Why is the LORD bringing us to this land only to let us fall by the sword? [Statement 2, anyone?] Our wives and children will be taken as plunder. Wouldn't it be better for us to go back to Egypt?" (Num. 13:26–14:3)

Look at the power of words! Not only did the bad report of a few turn into the grumbling of the masses, their grumblings in turn led to vain imaginations. By the time the faithless words rolled around in their heads a while, the men had already pictured themselves dead by the sword and their wives and children taken as plunder. Certainly our minds feed our mouths, but make no mistake — our mouths also feed our minds. We can talk ourselves not only into disbelief but into all manner of vain imaginations. Don't lose sight of the fact that these same people had seen no small evidence that . . .

> **God is who He says He is.**
> **God can do what He says He can do.**

To all but Joshua and Caleb, God may have been able to . . .

- send ten plagues, deliver them from the Egyptians (with plunder, no less),
- part the Red Sea,
- then swallow Pharaoh and his army in it,
- lead them with a cloud by day and a fire by night, and
- feed them with manna from heaven.

But He couldn't do a thing about those pesky Canaanites.

No wonder Moses and Aaron were so horrified by the rapid-fire unbelief that they "fell facedown in front of the whole Israelite assembly" (Num. 14:5).

If you and I want to abide and flourish in our Promised Lands, we're going to have to get rid of some bad reporting, faithless talking, and negative grumbling.

Later in the chapter, Moses pled with God to forgive the sins of the people "in accordance with [his] great love" (Num. 14:19). God's response causes the hair on the back of my neck to stand up. "I have forgiven them, as you asked. Nevertheless, as surely as I live and as surely as the glory of the LORD fills the whole earth, not one of the men who saw my glory and the miraculous signs I performed in Egypt and in the desert but who disobeyed me and tested me ten times — not one of them will ever see the land I promised on oath to their forefathers" (Num. 14:20–23).

If you and I want to abide and flourish in our Promised Lands, we're going to have to get rid of some bad reporting, faithless talking, and negative grumbling. In the previous chapter we learned that words wield power. While God's words are omnipotent, our words are potent because He created us in His image. We can tear down with our words or build up with our words. We can speak living words, or we can speak killing words. We can encourage, or we can discourage. The question is not whether our words affect; the question is how. Even if you're a quiet person, you still communicate often through words and just as often through affecting words.

You and I want to function in the full throttle of power God desires to give us. A significant portion of that power involves our mouths. Ideally, our faith can become voice and our voice can become the right kind of power when we're operating in the will of God. Just think how many activities involve the mouth and how eternally affecting our speech could become in everyday situations under God's control.

Every conversation does not have to be blatantly spiritual for God to make it positively effectual. Sometimes God gives us favor with people who are touched or impressed with how we express ourselves because God empowered our words even when the listener couldn't distinguish the difference. For months I've small-talked with a beautiful Indian woman, a Muslim, who works at my neighborhood dry cleaners. Just the other day she leaned over the counter with surprising warmth and asked, "Mrs. Moore, what do you do [for a living]?" I was able to tell her that I was once a very troubled person and that Christ had changed my life. I told her that He taught me how to live victoriously through studying the Bible and that I write books and give speeches in hopes of encouraging others to find life in Him as well. To my delight, she was very touched. I believe she wasn't turned off because the timing was right.

God had been laying the groundwork for a spiritual conversation for months. God intrigued this precious woman through simple small talk and graciously gave me favor with her. I can't wait to see what may develop. You also have countless occasions for God to turn what seems to be meaningless chatter into powerful affecting expression. Consider each of the following scenarios as opportunities, then think of the difference God's intervening power could make:

- Encouraging a friend on the phone or a coworker at the office
- Handling a difficult situation (or person!) at work
- Resolving a conflict
- Explaining a decision or a difficult concept
- Giving a presentation at school or at work
- Praying for someone
- Speaking a blessing over someone
- Teaching a class
- Offering someone advice or counsel
- Communicating with your mate
- Instructing your children
- Sharing and conversing with your children
- Sharing your testimony
- Mentoring someone
- Conversing with someone from a different generation
- Conversing with someone of a totally different culture

- Conversing with someone who doesn't know Christ
- Witnessing to someone about faith in Christ
- Preaching a sermon
- Offering an invitation for someone to receive Christ as Savior
- Worshipping and praising God

Communication is the essence of relationship, and words are its clearest means. Imagine what could happen if we allowed God to take authority of our mouths and infuse our words with His power. Think about the positive impact we could have on our circumstances, our mates, our children, our neighbors, coworkers, friends, and those we serve.

Scripture tells us that if Christ's words are dwelling in us, the Holy Spirit will often effect powerful results when we pray and speak what we believe. God may bring forth those results through different means and timetables than we pictured, but His Word says power is applied when we pray or speak in His name with faith. When we're actively trying to do what God says we can and consistently don't get the results God's Word says we can expect, we are wise to consider possible obstacles. If we often pray and "believe and therefore speak" yet our words continue to bear little fruit, the hindrance could be an unsanctified tongue. You'll see what I mean in a few moments.

As we consider this potential power blockage, please keep in mind that our goal is to identify and remove hindrances to practicing the powerful voice God's Word tells us we can. Feeling guilty or defeated is not the goal. Whenever we are confronted by a hard truth, God's purposes are always redemptive. In our previous chapter I quoted some passages from James 3 concerning the tongue. Take a look at another:

"With the tongue we praise our Lord and Father, and with it we curse men, who have been made in God's likeness. Out of the same mouth come praise and cursing. My brothers [and sisters], this should not be. Can both fresh water and salt water flow from the same spring?" (James 3:9–11).

When we believe therefore we speak, the Holy Spirit can use our tongues as instruments or vessels of supernatural power and bring about stunning results.

When Christ empowered His disciples to speak under His authority and effect certain results, He treated the tongue as an instrument. The muscle itself has no supernatural power. The understanding is that the Holy Spirit infuses power through the instrument. Likewise when we *believe therefore we speak* (2 Cor. 4:13), the Holy Spirit can use our tongues as instruments or vessels of supernatural power and bring about stunning results, whether immediately or over time. God is not, however, nearly as likely to powerfully and regularly infuse an instrument that is also employed for opposing purposes. In other words, the wrong use of the instrument can dramatically hinder its effectiveness with the right use.

You and I want to be people to whom God can entrust a spiritually powerful voice. Let's allow the Holy Spirit to alert us to some misuses of the tongue that can greatly diffuse its spiritual effectiveness:

- Gossip
- Lying
- Profanity
- Perversity
- Rudeness, unkindness, or disrespect
- Criticism
- Breaking a confidence
- Negativism and complaining
- Inappropriate humor, including off-color jokes or humor that demeans people

- Misuse of God's name

The costs of misusing God's name are probably incalculable. I'm not only talking about taking God's name in vain but using it loosely, inappropriately, or too casually. We can only imagine how reluctant God might be to infuse our prayers or statements said in His name when we have a tendency to misuse that same name.

Beloved, no matter how stubborn the tongue nor how habitual our problem, God can sanctify it and make it a vessel of honor and power. I wish I could turn up the volume on this next statement, so I ask you to hear it loud: No sin, no matter how momentarily pleasurable, comforting, or habitual, is worth missing what God has for us. Sin can undoubtedly cost us our earthly destinies. Yes, even sins of our mouths. Remember, Luke 6:45 says, "For out of the overflow of his heart his mouth speaks." A wayward tongue signals a wayward heart.

At various times and in various ways, all of us have blessed in one breath and cursed in the next. As well, we've all been tempted to talk one way in our spiritual relationships and another way in our worldly relationships. Inconsistency may be common, but it is also costly. We pay the price with powerlessness more often than we know. Lasting change demands prayer and attentive determination because bad habits are not easily broken. The dividends, however, are huge. Daily dependency on God develops unmatched intimacy, and a clean mouth unplugs a primary pipe of divine power. Furthermore, living with less regret of hastily spoken words is freedom indeed! Imagine the liberty of not having to worry about someone discovering we broke a confidence or talked unkindly behind her back. God's way is always the path of freedom.

No sin, no matter how momentarily pleasurable, comforting, or habitual, is worth missing what God has for us.

The tongue's potential to wreak havoc is staggering, yet so is its potential to reap the stuff of heaven on the turf of earth. We can rest assured God and Satan are both vying for authority over our mouths. Nothing is a greater threat to the enemy than a believer with the Word of God living and active upon her tongue, readily applied to any situation. If no part of the body is harder to submit to godly authority than the tongue (James 3:2), what could possess more power to reap benefit than one He controls? I know a wonderful place we could go to consecrate our mouths to God. Come with me to the glorious scene depicted in Isaiah 6:1–8.

In the year that King Uzziah died, I saw the Lord seated on a throne, high and exalted, and the train of his robe filled the temple. Above him were seraphs, each with six wings: With two wings they covered their faces, with two they covered their feet, and with two they were flying. And they were calling to one another:

"Holy, holy, holy is the LORD
Almighty;
the whole earth is full of his glory."

At the sound of their voices the doorposts and thresholds shook and the temple was filled with smoke.

"Woe to me!" I cried. "I am ruined! For I am a man of unclean lips, and I live among a people of unclean lips, and my eyes have seen the King, the LORD Almighty."

Then one of the seraphs flew to me with a live coal in his hand, which he had taken with tongs from the altar. With it he touched my mouth and said, "See, this has touched your lips; your guilt is taken away and your sin atoned for."

Then I heard the voice of the Lord saying, "Whom shall I send? And who will go for us?"

And I said, "Here am I. Send me!"

As sophisticated as we'd like to think we are, we have more in common with the ancient prophet Isaiah than we might admit. Unless you are highly unusual, your tongue — just like mine — has been misused and misappropriated countless times. As if our own tendencies aren't bad enough, we also live among a people of unclean lips. Many of us live or work in environments where backbiting, gossip, lying, profanity, and off-color remarks and jokes are pandemic. Like Isaiah, God wants to send you and me forth into our worlds in His name. The instrument of His greatest potential use in each of our lives is the tongue. No, we're not all called to speak, teach, or preach, but we are all called to use our mouths to glorify His name.

Recall once more how many of Christ's New Testament commands involve the tongue. We've been called to share Jesus with the lost and give our testimonies any time we have the opportunity to tell another person of our hope. We've been called to pray. Yes, we *can* and *do* pray silently, but not coincidentally some of our most explosively powerful praying will be aloud. We've been called to disciple others, teaching God's Word and His ways. We've been called to encourage the hopeless and weary. *And,* Beloved, we've also been called to speak to some mountains and tell them to "Move!"

A wayword tongue
signals a wayword heart.

Too much power is at stake to continue cultivating an inconsistent and unconsecrated mouth. The challenge of a tamed tongue is so great that we'd be wise to give it daily attention in prayer, but I'm asking God to perform a powerful and memorable work today. Through God's Word and prayer, let's go to the throne of grace like Isaiah did. Look back at the passages from Isaiah 6 once more.

Nothing is more important in the atoning scene of Isaiah's vision than the altar from which the live coal was taken.

The original word for *altar* in this segment comes from a Hebrew word translated *sacrifice*. Other kinds of altars existed among the ancient people. The altar of incense was also in the temple, but I believe the live coals in this vision could only have been removed from the altar of sacrifice. Why? Because coals, no matter how consumed with fire, have no power to take away guilt or atone for sin. I am convinced that the God-appointed power the coals had to purge and atone came from the blood of the sacrifice laid upon the altar. God's Word never veers from the concept that all remission of sins comes through the shedding of sacrificial blood (Heb. 9:22).

Jesus Christ graced earth's guilty sod to offer Himself as the perfect sacrifice and fulfill every requirement of the Law once and for all. He shed His precious blood on an altar constructed of two pieces of wood and fashioned into a cross. The fire of holy judgment met with the blood of the spotless Lamb, and our guilt was purged and our sins atoned. Glory to His name! We need no further act of atonement, but we are desperate for the continuing work of sanctification.

Today you and I stand before the same throne the prophet Isaiah approached in his glorious vision. God is just as holy. Just as high and lifted up. The train of His robe still fills the temple, and the seraphs still cry "Holy!" But the writer of Hebrews 4:15–16 tells us that because we have Jesus as our great High Priest, we boldly approach a throne of *grace*. The same grace that saves also sanctifies, and we could use a fresh work of consecration, couldn't we? In one way or another, we, too, are a people of unclean lips, and we undoubtedly live among a people of unclean lips. How God wants to use our mouths! But He is calling us to a fresh consecration and a willingness to turn from misuse. Today could be that day. Tarry with Him at the altar. Make confession and petition.

We need not hang our heads and beg. All we need to do is lift up our faces and ask. May Jesus touch our lips again with coals from the altar and set our tongues aflame with His holy fire.

"What do these stones mean?"

Joshua 4:6

Chapter Twelve

Believing God
Was Faithful in Your Past

You and I have talked about our Promised Lands from the beginning of this book. We started our journey at the Jordan water's edge looking in the distance to our Canaan, the land where we've been called to walk by faith and fulfill our divine destinies. Our land of promise is the place we abide, actively and presently believing God. It is a good land. A land of harvest. Through the chapters of this book and the prescribed faith practices, I pray that you and I have been moving step-by-step across the dry riverbed with the waters of the Jordan heaped to each side.

In our present chapter I'd like to meet you in the middle of the riverbed to draw out some stones and stand them up as memorials. The middle of any challenging journey can be the most critical point.

Many of us may not be where we were, but we're not yet where we want to go. Perhaps the terrible bondage of Egypt is behind us, but the land of promise seems remote. The longer we wander in the wilderness between, the greater the chance we'll return to captivity. The pull of familiar comforts and habits can feel overpowering, particularly against the uncertainty of Canaan's unknowns. You and I may need a little extra motivation to press ahead. Appropriately, we'll find that motivation embedded as solid rock right in the middle of the Jordan. Picture the scene as you read Joshua 4:1–18:

> When the whole nation had finished crossing the Jordan, the LORD said to Joshua, "Choose twelve men from among the people, one from each tribe, and tell them to take up twelve stones from the middle of the Jordan from right where the priests stood and to carry them over with you and put them down at the place where you stay tonight."
> So Joshua called together the twelve men he had appointed from the Israelites, one from each tribe, and said to them, "Go over before

the ark of the LORD your God into the middle of the Jordan. Each of you is to take up a stone on his shoulder, according to the number of the tribes of the Israelites, to serve as a sign among you. In the future, when your children ask you, 'What do these stones mean?' tell them that the flow of the Jordan was cut off before the ark of the covenant of the LORD. When it crossed the Jordan, the waters of the Jordan were cut off. These stones are to be a memorial to the people of Israel forever."

So the Israelites did as Joshua commanded them. They took the twelve stones from the middle of the Jordan, according to the number of the tribes of the Israelites, as the LORD had told Joshua; and they carried them over with them to their camp, where they put them down. Joshua set up the twelve stones that had been in the middle of the Jordan at the spot where the priests who carried the ark of the covenant had stood. And they are there to this day.

Now the priests who carried the

ark remained standing in the middle of the Jordan until everything the LORD had commanded Joshua was done by the people, just as Moses had directed Joshua. The people hurried over, and as soon as all of them had crossed, the ark of the LORD and the priests came to the other side while the people watched. The men of Reuben, Gad, and the half-tribe of Manasseh crossed over, armed, in front of the Israelites, as Moses had directed them. About forty thousand armed for battle crossed over before the LORD to the plains of Jericho for war.

That day the LORD exalted Joshua in the sight of all Israel; and they revered him all the days of his life, just as they had revered Moses.

Then the LORD said to Joshua, "Command the priests carrying the ark of the Testimony to come up out of the Jordan."

So Joshua commanded the priests, "Come up out of the Jordan."

And the priests came up out of the river carrying the ark of the covenant of the LORD. No sooner had they set their feet on dry ground than the waters of the Jordan returned to their place and ran at flood stage as before.

Can you imagine the crashing roar of the closing waters as the last few children of Israel stepped out of the Jordan? Joshua 4:10 tells us "the people hurried over." With a wall of water suspended on each side of them, I'll bet! Surely God has all these scenes videotaped for us in heaven, and we'll finally have the sound effects to go with the screenplay. Until then, use your imagination on dramatic scenes like this. Every now and then a friend teases me about being a drama queen. I don't deny it, but I also don't mind saying that God is the ultimate drama King. He didn't have to make biblical scenes exciting. He could have achieved His will by compulsory methodic order. I'd like to suggest that God Himself enjoys the drama. Everything about the Israelites' Promised Land adventure was electrifying, even when it was terrifying. Yours is liable to be similar. God's pathways to promise are anything but boring.

Every command of God has great purpose, even when man struggles to discern it. He left no question why the Israelites were to take twelve stones from the middle of the Jordan however. Joshua 4:7 explains, "These stones are to be a memorial to the people of Israel forever." In other words, God and the children of Israel were about to share an experience He meant them never to forget.

A powerful motivation for believing God in our present is intentionally remembering how He's worked in our past.

Every now and then when we are about to experience something new and even unsettling, I'll say to my children, "We're about to make a memory." A romantic at heart, I dearly love making memories. At least a hundred scenes are like murals brushed on the walls of my mind in technicolor paint. Through memory I can still "see" exactly what Amanda looked like when we shared our first moment alone in my hospital room. I will also treasure the indelible scene when Melissa was presented before our church after she surrendered to ministry. I will also picture Keith with a smoking shotgun in his hand and a dead rattlesnake at my feet as long as I live.

Some moments are worthy to be memorialized. In fact, even a difficult or challenging situation is more palatable to me if I know instinctively that something memorable is bound to come from it.

As the people of Israel stood at the river's edge, they were about to make a memory with God. As He looked on the scene of parted waters and promises kept, I wonder if a certain mural painted on the walls of His mind seemed suddenly fluorescent. God prescribed a specific response to the Israelites when their children and descendants asked the question, "What do these stones mean?"

"Tell them that the flow of the Jordan was cut off before the ark of the covenant of the LORD. When it crossed the Jordan, the waters of the Jordan were cut off. These stones are to be a memorial to the people of Israel forever."

The Hebrew transliteration for "cut off" is *karat* meaning "to cut, cut off; to make a covenant."[6] The term could be used for any kind of cutting, but it can represent much more when placed in the context with covenant. If we could read Hebrew, we'd see how often the Old Testament speaks of God not only forming a covenant but "cutting covenant." The obvious tie is that God often represented the terms of the covenant through a sacrifice. The first time God ever dictated perimeters of the Promised Land in Scripture is in perfect context with covenant. In Genesis 15, the Lord commanded Abram to bring Him a heifer, a goat, and a ram and "cut them in two and arrange the halves opposite each other." He then placed Abram in a deep sleep and prophesied the four-hundred-year captivity in Egypt. Take a close look at Genesis 15:17–21.

"When the sun had set and darkness had fallen, a smoking firepot with a blazing torch appeared and passed between the pieces. On that day the LORD made [*karat*, "cut"] a covenant with Abram and said, 'To your descendants I give this land, from the river of Egypt to the great river, the Euphrates — the land of the Kenites, Kenizzites, Kadmonites, Hittites, Perizzites, Rephaites, Amorites, Canaanites, Girgashites and Jebusites.' "

God's prophecies found their fulfillment to the Israelites much later through four hundred years of Egyptian captivity followed by a great deliverance. As the events of the book of Joshua unfolded, we can be sure the eyes of the El Roi (the God who sees) were fastened upon the faithful fulfillment of His promises to His chosen nation. Joshua 4:7 tells us that "the flow of the Jordan was cut off [*karat*, "to cut, cut off; to make a covenant"] before the ark of the covenant of the LORD." Scripture specifies that when "it crossed the Jordan, the waters of the Jordan were cut off [*karat*]." "It" refers to the ark of the covenant also called "the ark of God, which is called by the Name, the name of the LORD Almighty, who is enthroned between the cherubim that are on the ark" (2 Sam. 6:2).

In reference to the crossing of the Jordan River, God said in Deuteronomy 31:3, "The LORD your God himself will cross over ahead of you." In the scene depicted in Joshua 4, I wonder if the waters ultimately parted for the presence of God Himself who crossed over ahead of the Israelites. I also wonder if God had a memorial moment all His own when He looked upon those parted waters and remembered that first covenant and the path cut so He could keep His promises.

God never forgets His promises to us. In turn, He intends for His children never to forget His faithfulness to fulfill them. Over and over in Scripture, God's people are told to actively remember all He has done on their behalf. In fact, the practice of remembering is so important to the children of God that He often diagnosed their seasons of rebellion as serious cases of forgetfulness. See a couple of examples for yourself:

When our fathers were in Egypt, they gave no thought to your miracles; they did not remember your many kindnesses, and they rebelled by the sea, the Red Sea. (Ps. 106:7)

Then they believed his promises and sang his praise. But they soon forgot what he had done and did not wait for his counsel. (Ps. 106:12–13)

A powerful motivation for believing God in our present is intentionally remembering how He's worked in our past. Earlier I talked about memories I've made with my family that seem engraved on my mind forever. My relationship with God, however, preceded my present family and proceeded long after my mother died. In other words, my longest and most effectual history with anyone has been with God Himself. I received Christ as my Savior in childhood and have loved Him longer, known Him better, and experienced life with Him more intimately than with anyone else. I assure you, God and I have made some memories together. Hard ones. Good ones. Astounding ones. You don't have to know God long to make memories with Him. If you got deeply involved with Him when you came to know Him, you have a memorable history with God no matter how brief your relationship through Christ has been. The more you look back, the more you can see that He was also at work long before you accepted His Son as your Savior. You have made some memories with God. He has undoubtedly been faithful to you, and your active remembrance of His faithfulness yesterday will greatly increase your willingness to trust Him today.

The memorial stones drawn from the riverbed were meant to be visible reminders of God's faithfulness to the Israelites. We could use a few ourselves, so let's apply the analogy our own way. In order to strengthen our faith muscles, we're going to exert a little energy reflecting upon and memorializing times when God has openly demonstrated His faithfulness to us. Think of the path through the Jordan River as the step-by-step process through which God has taken us to lead us to our own Promised Lands. See where you can retrace God and remember His goodness to you. Perhaps you've never forgotten many of His faithful acts, but have you ever literally recorded them? Will your children and your descendants, whether physical or spiritual, have any kind of written record of their lineage and heritage of faith?

Melissa made a very hard decision to transfer from a well-known Texas university to a tremendous institution for biblical training after her sophomore year of college. The choice was costly. She lost a year of hard-earned academic hours, moved far away from home, and settled into a crowded dorm without knowing a single person. I keep thinking about something she said to me as her voice choked over the difficult decision. "When I teach my children to follow hard after God no matter where He takes them, I want them to know that their mother does what she teaches." From many miles away I've watched her make memories with God. He has done things for her that Mom and Dad are no longer near enough to do. She not only took a step of faith for herself, she took one for her physical and spiritual descendants.

Psalm 77:11–12 says, "I will remember the deeds of the LORD; yes, I will remember your miracles of long ago. I will meditate on all your works and consider all your mighty deeds." If you're willing to participate, I'd like to ask you to join me in personalizing the psalmist's words and apply his historical reference to "long ago" to your own personal "long ago." We're going to glance back and see what treasures we can find, sometimes even in the midst of rubble. Like detectives at a scene, start looking for any visible fingerprints of your invisible God interspersed throughout your life. Beloved, God has been there all along, even before you acknowledged Him as Savior. He is the infinite, eternal omnipresent God who woos to His heart those who will draw near. It's time for some positive memory retrieval, Dear Ones! The kind that edifies rather than terrifies.

God has been there all along,
even before you acknowledged
Him as Savior.

Meditate on the *World Book Encyclopedia*'s offering on the subject of remembering: "Memory is a vital part of the learning process. Without it, learning would be impossible. If your brain recorded nothing from the past, you would be unable to learn anything new. All your experiences would be lost as soon as they ended and each new situation would be totally unfamiliar. Without memory, you would repeatedly have the same experiences for the 'first time.' Memory gives a richness to life — the pleasures of happy remembrances as well as the sorrow of unhappy ones."[7]

Imagine all the spiritual implications of an active memory in our walk with God. Without a doubt, memory is a vital part of the learning process, and it is also a vital part of the faith-building process. Perhaps you're already trying to think back over your past and recall specific evidences of God's activity. Though you may be convinced He's been there for you all along, you may be drawing a mental blank on many precise instances. That's OK. We are going to enlist the help of the Holy Spirit in remembering and recording acts of God's faithfulness to us in the span of our lifetimes. John 14:26 intimates a role He fulfills that can greatly assist us. As Christ prepared His disciples for His absence, He gave them this assurance:

"But the Counselor, the Holy Spirit, whom the Father will send in my name, will teach you all things and will remind you of everything I have said to you."

When you and I received Christ, the Spirit of God took up immediate residency inside of us. He has many roles, but one targeted in this verse can be most involved in the task before us. The Holy Spirit is the blessed Reminder. He can as easily remind us of what we've experienced with God as He can remind us of what we've been taught. I love the companion role suggested in the same verse. The Holy Spirit is also our able Counselor. Often He works through spiritually gifted human agents, but in terms of the exercises I'm suggesting, many of you will find He's all you need. Our purpose is not to provoke deeply embedded, traumatic memories but to quicken the memory of God's faithful provision and revealed presence along the way.

Please consider spending some time in prayer over the coming days (even weeks if necessary) toward the goal of remembering God. Ask Him to cause His Holy Spirit to remind you of the works of Jesus throughout your life: His presence, His activity, and many of the things He has taught and revealed to you along your journey. Like a river spilling into the sea, actively remembering God in our past spills into believing God for our future. Beloved, whether or not we're able to discover palpable evidences, we can be certain God was faithful even when we were faithless (2 Tim. 2:13).

He was making Godstops long before we started to notice.

I have provided a time line for you at the end of this chapter that I hope you'll complete as a personalized record of your faith walk. The following suggestions will hopefully spark some vivid memories and help you organize your thoughts:

1. Record your birthday on the bold dot that begins the time line at the bottom of the page. Remember, God was already at work in your life before you were born, so if you know anything significant that happened in your family line to give you a heritage of faith, record it in words or brief phrases in the margin preceding the dot. For instance, one of your grandparents may have been a missionary or Sunday school teacher. A heritage of faith can also come to us in less traditional ways. I have a friend whose grandfather was a murderer who had a radical conversion to Christ, deeply affecting his family line. Sometimes negatives can have an even deeper impact on a future life of faith than positives. Record anything that might qualify as an invitation to a life of faith.

2. At the end of the time line, you will find a bold dot that is followed by ". . .". The ". . ." obviously represents your fu-

ture. Over the preceding single bold dot toward the top of the page, please record your present age as well as the month and year that you are reading this book so that you can date it as the present.

3. The time line is divided into five segments to help you organize your thoughts. Take your present age and divide it by five, then write the age or approximate age you were at each of those dividers. Use my time line as an example. As I pen these

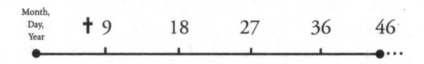

pages, I am 46. Since 45 divides more evenly by five, I'd approximate by writing 9, 18, 27, and 36 over the dividing lines. According to Step 2, I've already written 46 over my concluding bold dot.

4. If you have received Christ as your personal Savior, approximate the point when you became a Christian on the time line and identify it with a †. Because I have a very sketchy memory of my early childhood, I don't remember the exact time of my conversion. But I know that by the time I was eight or nine, the Holy Spirit seemed actively at work in my life,

convicting me of sin and stirring in me a longing to know and please God; therefore, I'm marking my time line with the cross at about that age. You may do likewise if you are not entirely sure. Ask yourself how long have you been certain you were a Christian, then mark your line with a cross at that beginning point.

5. Take the next days or several weeks to fill in the time line at the end of the chapter with significant events or obvious moves and interventions of God that in retrospect proved vital in a future walk of faith. The five age segments should help you organize your thoughts as you recall those periods of your life. Represent significant events or faithful acts of God by writing dots on the line and identifying words or phrases above them. Think of these dots as your memorial stones or stones of remembrance drawn from your Jordan. Some of you may think at first that you don't have a walk of faith. Beloved, something has caused you to pick up a book of this kind and read this far. God is drawing you. Very likely you will be able to look back over the course of what may have even been a difficult life and see where He planted people and events to move you toward Him. I had a difficult

childhood, a turbulent adolescence, and an erratic young adulthood, yet I can still see God's provision and intervention as He drew me step-by-step to Himself. Somehow the painful years can provide a contrasting backdrop that makes the activity of God even more obvious.

Again, your stones are to represent spiritual markers or anything of significance that ultimately led to a walk of faith. Allow the following questions to provoke some memories of events that proved important over time.

Did any relocations or moves occur that God used to draw you closer to Himself?

Did any births or deaths occur that proved significant to your faith walk over time? (Remember to document even negative or difficult events if God ultimately or immediately used them to draw, reach, or teach you.)

Did God plant anyone in your life for a season of time who had a great impact on you? Document the beginning of that relationship.

Did you attend a Bible school, camp, revival, or conference that became life changing to you?

Did any kind of event, whether positive or negative, have a significant effect on a future faith walk? (Consider events such as promotions or layoffs, a sickness or surprising recovery. You may recall that I have mentioned a crisis season of my life in my early thirties. This period of time was undoubtedly the most disastrous season of my adult life, but it finds a crucial place on my time line because God used it so dramatically to break and remake me. You may have a similar season that needs to be documented on your time line.)

Have you been baptized? By all means, document that vital memorial stone on your time line.

I hope you're getting the idea. More than anything, this time line is yours. Tailor it any way that makes the most sense to you. Beloved, you have a story. A "Hisstory." After you document your history with God on this time line, maybe you'll decide to go further and actually journal these events with a descriptive written record. That's your call. The point is that you have made memories with God. Let them stand as memorial stones not only for you but for your physical or spiritual descendants. When the future looks tough, glance back at your standing stones and be reminded once again: God is ever faithful to you.

Month,
Day,
Year

Then the LORD said to Joshua,
"Today I have rolled away the
reproach of Egypt from you."

Joshua 5:9

So the place has been called
Gilgal to this day.

Chapter Thirteen

Believing God to Get You to Your Gilgal

In this chapter we have the opportunity to meet at a strategic place that I pray holds something significant for each of us. Join me in Gilgal. Remember, firsts are always important. As you read these passages, note the timing and the events that took place at the first stop east of the Jordan.

> On the tenth day of the first month the people went up from the Jordan and camped at Gilgal on the eastern border of Jericho. And Joshua set up at Gilgal the twelve stones they had taken out of the Jordan. . . .
>
> At that time the LORD said to Joshua, "Make flint knives and circumcise the Israelites again." So Joshua made flint knives and circumcised the Israelites at Gibeath Haaraloth.

Now this is why he did so: All those who came out of Egypt — all the men of military age — died in the desert on the way after leaving Egypt. All the people that came out had been circumcised, but all the people born in the desert during the journey from Egypt had not. The Israelites had moved about in the desert forty years until all the men who were of military age when they left Egypt had died, since they had not obeyed the LORD. For the LORD had sworn to them that they would not see the land that he had solemnly promised their fathers to give us, a land flowing with milk and honey. So he raised up their sons in their place, and these were the ones Joshua circumcised. They were still uncircumcised because they had not been circumcised on the way. And after the whole nation had been circumcised, they remained where they were in camp until they were healed.

Then the Lord said to Joshua, "Today I have rolled away the reproach of Egypt from you." So the place has been called Gilgal to this day.

On the evening of the fourteenth day of the month, while camped at Gilgal on the plains of Jericho, the Israelites celebrated the Passover. The day after the Passover, that very day, they ate some of the produce of the land: unleavened bread and roasted grain. The manna stopped the day after they ate this food from the land; there was no longer any manna for the Israelites, but that year they ate of the produce of Canaan. (Josh. 4:19–20; 5:2–12)

God's penchant for good timing is beautifully illustrated in the nation of Israel's first true occupation of the land of promise. Not coincidentally, the Israelites passed through the Jordan and set up camp in Gilgal just in time to celebrate the Passover. In fact, the children of Israel "went up from the Jordan and camped at Gilgal" on "the tenth day of the first month," a very important anniversary. Back in Exodus 12 God gave instructions to the enslaved Israelites how to prepare for that very first Passover, the precursor to their deliverance. Exodus 12:3 reads: "Tell the whole community of Israel that on the tenth day of [the first month] each man is to take a lamb for his family, one for each household."

Forty years later the Israelites emerged from the Jordan on that memorial day. If you'll listen closely with spiritual ears, you might even hear the bleating of the sheep as the Israelites used their rods and staffs to guide them through the parted waters. Four days later the Israelites celebrated their first Passover in the Promised Land. The original Passover they memorialized was intended for their immediate deliverance and swift entrance into Canaan. Their unbelief, however, led to a desert full of carcasses and four decades of wanderings. Finally, the Israelites made it. I don't believe any coincidence can be blamed for the name card the Word gives to the location of their first camp.

In essence, the word *Gilgal* means "circle or wheel." The assumption is that the standing stones were arranged in a circle, but I think another rich application also emerges. I believe Gilgal could also represent the place where the Hebrew nation came full circle. God strategically timed the crossing on the memorial anniversary of the preparations for the first Passover as if God might have been saying, "Let's try this again." Equally significant, Gilgal was the location in the Promised Land where

God commanded the men to be circumcised, reconfirming the sign of covenant they were to bear. The covenant mark of circumcision had been neglected throughout the wilderness wanderings.

God's timing presented the Israelites with a major do-over, and this time they did it right. God put it His own way in Joshua 5:9. After they walked by faith through the parted waters and obeyed Him through circumcision, the Lord said, "Today I have rolled away the reproach of Egypt from you." The text then explains, "So the place has been called Gilgal to this day." If we could read Hebrew, we'd see how often God performs a play on words. This Scripture provides one of many examples. "Rolled away" is the Hebrew transliteration of *galal,* obviously similar in form and sound to the word *gilgal. Galal* means "to roll, turn, drive away; to be rolled together, roll oneself upon; to be rolled (in blood), be dyed red."[8] God rolled away (*galal*) their reproach as if on a wheel (*gilgal*), thereby breaking their old cycle and bringing them full circle. The circular monument of stones stood as a lasting memorial.

I'd like to suggest that Gilgal is an important place for you and me to go with

God as well. Think of your personal Gilgal as the place where two highly significant works occur:

1. God brings you full circle and breaks any looming cycle of failure.
2. God rolls away your reproach.

We know we're coming full circle with God when we stand at a very similar crossroad where we made such a mess of life before, but this time we take a different road!

First, let's talk about old cycles and coming full circle. I lived so much of my life in a cycle of defeat that this subject is familiar to me. I describe my history of defeat as cyclical because I did not remain indefinitely in a pit. As I shared with you earlier, I really did have a heart for God, however unhealthy it may have been. My sin would always bring heartbreak, and I'd confess and repent with all the energy I had. I'd crawl out of the pit with dirt under my nails rather than allow God to lift me out by His loving grace. Because I hadn't allowed God to heal my wounded heart or ever believed I was who He said I was, sooner or later I'd cycle back into another pit.

Every believer needs second chances. Some of us need lots of them. God looks upon our hearts and knows whether we have any authentic desire to be different or if we're all talk. When lasting change finally comes, few things are as healing as evidence that the cycle is breaking. We may have the same old struggles, but we're making some new decisions. We know we're coming full circle with God when we stand at a very similar crossroad where we made such a mess of life before, but this time we take a different road.

At the water's edge, the nation of Israel faced a do-over. Surely they couldn't look at that heap of water without recalling what had happened forty years earlier when they were children. They had been in a situation like this once before. After observing their first Passover, the Red Sea stood between them and freedom. God parted those mighty waters, and Israelites passed through on dry ground . . . only to fall into a wilderness drought of unbelief. At the Jordan they received a new opportunity through parted waters. They could remain in the wilderness or proceed to their Promised Land by faith. Choosing to believe, they made the right decision — perfectly timed for a victorious observance of

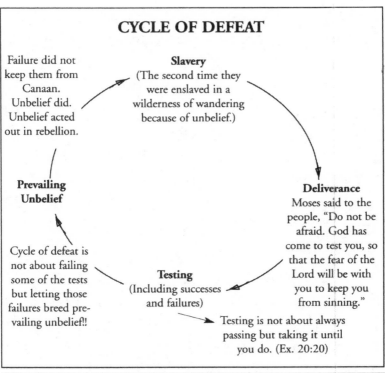

CYCLE OF DEFEAT

Slavery
(The second time they were enslaved in a wilderness of wandering because of unbelief.)

Failure did not keep them from Canaan. Unbelief did. Unbelief acted out in rebellion.

Prevailing Unbelief

Cycle of defeat is not about failing some of the tests but letting those failures breed prevailing unbelief!!

Testing
(Including successes and failures)

Deliverance
Moses said to the people, "Do not be afraid. God has come to test you, so that the fear of the Lord will be with you to keep you from sinning."

Testing is not about always passing but taking it until you do. (Ex. 20:20)

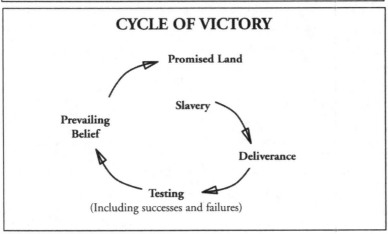

CYCLE OF VICTORY

Promised Land

Slavery

Prevailing Belief

Deliverance

Testing
(Including successes and failures)

Passover. The old cycle was broken, and a new cycle ushered them into their destiny.

Are you like me? Have you lived much of your life in a repetitious cycle? Perhaps we can recognize our own personal cycles more easily by viewing a paradigm of Israel's. Here are two of the most common cycles of defeat and victory. Note the similar beginnings but very different endings and the crucial point of departure.

As you can see, both cycles begin with some kind of slavery. Scripture is clear that all people have been enslaved to sin. Mind you, slavery takes on all sorts of forms. We can be enslaved by anything — from determined disbelief, to victory-robbing timidity, to all manner of physical or sexual addictions/compulsions. Slavery is anything that keeps you bound from your God-ordained destiny and the fulfillment of His earthward promises to you.

Deeper in each cycle, perhaps many of us have experienced a deliverance of some kind. Certainly those who are believers in Christ have been delivered from a general and otherwise hopeless bondage to sin. Christians can also unfortunately experience areas of captivity long after conversion. My personal history of deliverance began when I accepted Christ as Savior;

but since that time He has also delivered me from tremendous insecurity, much fear, very defeated thinking, and self-destructive practices of sin. In all likelihood you've also experienced deliverance of one kind or another.

Let's go to the next step on each cycle. Everyone who has been delivered from some area of bondage has also experienced times of testing. In the previous chapter we talked about remembering versus forgetting God. Which we decide to do falls under this segment of the cycle. Whether we'll forget God's faithfulness to us is definitely among the tests we're sure to face. Whatever the course exam, the outcome of the pop quizzes preparing us for it may include both our successes and failures. I believe God continues to test us in an area until we pass. Sometimes He even seems to insist on an A. Ultimately, how the cycle continues is based on one of two things: prevailing unbelief or prevailing belief.

The word *prevailing* is important because few Christians will operate entirely in the extreme of no belief or unwavering belief. God does not sit upon His throne with a flyswatter waiting to smack us at the first hint of doubt. Keith and I often say that we failed and flopped our way to faith, but somehow through the grace of God, we kept falling forward. As long as we wear these cumbersome suits of flesh, we are not going to be supermen flying high in the sky of faith. We are called to something far more elementary: to walk by faith. God most often looks for what prevails in our lives. If unbelief prevails, we find ourselves repeating the cycle of defeat. We may have different scenery but the pattern is the same.

Boy, have I been there. Yet, to the glory of God, not in a number of years. Belief finally prevailed, and the old cycle broke. He retested me in some past areas of defeat, and *finally* I began passing more than failing and believing more than disbelieving. Prevailing belief then led to a far more consistent state of abiding in my Promised Land. The same will be true for you on your own timetable with God. If you have not yet experienced what I'm describing, your Gilgal awaits you, and I pray you will not rest until God takes you there.

If you feel like you've been to Gilgal with God, then soberly consider with me that we can't presume to always remain there. Neither cycle noted on page 243 is necessarily permanent as long as we dwell on this earth. Our patterns or cycles can change and spiral up . . . or revert and spiral down. Unfortunately the Israelites did not abide in the freedom and prosperity of their Promised Land indefinitely. The idolatry and disobedience that later led to Assyrian and Babylonian captivity grew from roots of prevailing unbelief. You and I don't have to follow suit. The Spirit of the living Christ abides in us, bearing faithfulness as fruit (Gal. 5:22–23). We won't walk in perfect faith for the rest of our lives, but we can walk in prevailing faith.

I remember experiencing a Gilgal moment when I realized God had brought me full circle in an area of my life. The encounter was surreal. Having returned to my home state of Arkansas to lead a conference, I was introduced to a young woman at a tea. After telling me her name, our mutual friend explained, "She teaches your Bible studies at your old church in Arkadelphia." Time froze for me, and I recalled how defeated I felt as a young person. I sat on the pews of that church and walked down its halls in total defeat, having already made some very poor decisions. I was convinced everyone at the church lived in victory but me. I wore my reproach like letters on a sweater.

Many years passed and I experienced a

mixture of successes and failures, but God's stubborn love and call to faith finally prevailed. As the young woman stood before me, I could hardly assimilate the journey. I had returned to the church where I felt such shame but this time as a Bible study teacher via videotape. I did not know where life would take me from there, but I knew in that moment and in that one way it had come full circle. The pall of sin's bondage and death had passed over me. I had been to Gilgal. Beloved, God has a full-circle Gilgal for you too. And that's not all that awaits you there.

God has a second highly significant work to perform at your Gilgal. He wants to roll away all your reproach. You might take another glance at the segment of Scripture at the beginning of this chapter. You don't want to miss the fact that God rolled away Israel's reproach after reconfirming the rite of covenantal circumcision and observing their obedience to His command. I can't help but notice that a wounding of sorts took place before the Israelites were released to live fruitfully in their land of promise. Been there. So have many others. I don't know a single person who truly seems to bear the mark of God's presence and power in his or her life who hasn't been asked by God to be obedient in a way that was dramatically painful. A cutting away of sorts is almost always involved in a life moving toward the Promised Land.

Through the reconfirmation of the rite of circumcision, God in effect cut away the physical sign of their unbelief, then He rolled away their reproach. How does this concept apply to New Testament believers in Christ? Colossians 2:11–12 says, "In [Christ] you were also circumcised, in the putting off of the sinful nature, not with a circumcision done by the hands of men but with the circumcision done by Christ, having been buried with him in baptism and raised with him through your faith in the power of God, who raised him from the dead."

For the sake of our application, lay Ephesians 4:22 beside that passage and watch for our responsibility in the process. "You were taught with regard to your former way of life, to put off your old self, which is being corrupted by its deceitful desires; to be made new in the attitude of your minds."

Reproach is any feeling of shame, any sense that we've been despised or become the object of contempt.

Think of our reproach as the vestiges of what we still insisted on wearing from our old wardrobe, whether telltale actions occurred before or after our salvation. At the risk of being a bit graphic, it was that which Christ circumcised but we tried to keep as a cover. Our wardrobe problem (our unwillingness to "put off" some things we've been wearing) is a mental issue, really. Though we were totally changed on the inside when we were made new creatures in Christ, our minds often take time to be renewed. That's what Paul meant when he told us to be "made new in the attitude of your minds." We're far more likely to act like the old man of sin when we still feel like the old man of sin.

I'd like to suggest that every single one of us needs a trip to Gilgal in the course of our challenging lives because few of us "put off" every part of our old wardrobe completely and instantaneously. Not only do we insist on wearing some of our old wardrobe, sometimes we also insist on wearing pieces of other people's wardrobes. In other words, we can be victimized by someone else's reproach or simply take on something that was never ours.

The Old Testament Lexical Aids' definition of *reproach* will broaden our thinking and help us further relate: "Reproach, shame, scorn, contempt; the object of reproach. Has the connotation of blaming others, pointing the finger, a stigma. In a figurative sense, someone or something which is despised."[9]

Reproach can mean any kind of stigma that we feel we've worn along the way. For instance, anything we've done (or been) that could cause people to point an accusing finger at us. Reproach can be a feeling, real or imagined, of blame for something with serious consequences. Certainly reproach is any feeling of shame, any sense that we've been despised or become the object of contempt.

Many of you may remember *The Scarlet Letter*, one of the most familiar pieces of literature wardrobing its protagonist in a stigma or sign of reproach. **A** for adulterer is not the only letter a person can feel he or she wears as a stigma. Consider a few others that believers along the way have confirmed for me.

Do you by any chance feel like you wear a **D** for "divorced"? Perhaps the divorce was not your choice or, even if it was, it occurred twenty years ago. Still, you feel like you can't get out from under the stigma.

An **S** for "shamed"? From victimization?

Poor choices? Or, like me, both?

A **C** for "crazy"? I know people who have experienced a dreadful period of mental illness or emotional collapse and who now feel that observers will not let them out from under the stigma. I know someone who takes medication for a serious mental illness but will not tell anyone because she fears the stigma.

A **B** for "bankrupt"? Did you have to file years ago but still feel shamed by it?

An **F** for "fired"? Did you lose a job and end up feeling like you wore a big *F* on your sweater to every interview that followed?

An **H** for "harlot"? You've been living in victory for a while, but the accuser keeps telling you that you'll always be what you were?

An **L** for "lesbian," although you turned from that lifestyle several years ago?

An **H** for "homosexual" because the kids at school said you were effeminate?

A **TP** for "terrible parent" because one of your children rebelled or hurt himself somehow?

Has anyone worn a **DWI**?

Have you by any chance spent a night in jail and feel like you still wear a **JB** for "jailbird"?

A **U** for "unwanted" when in reality you are honorably single?

A **POM** for "pregnant outside marriage"? I have a friend with a precious fifteen-year-old who was conceived outside of marriage. God has redeemed this mother's life from a pit and given her a child who loves Jesus, yet my friend still feels like she wears a stigma. Can anyone relate?

The list of letters could go on and on. Some of us, myself at the front of the line, have even worn multiple letters. I looked like I spilled a bowl of alphabet soup on my sweater. Some of my letters weren't even real, but I was so convinced of the reproach that I pinned them on myself. What letters have you worn? If you have the courage and the privacy to write down your own letters in this space and what they stand for, you might be helped by having something specific to lay before God and lose once and for all.

Beloved, if you are still wearing any kind of reproach from your past and certainly if you are wearing something through victimization that never belonged on you, you need a trip to Gilgal. God is waiting for you there. He wants to remind you of the cross of Christ, your Passover Lamb (1

Cor. 5:7), and memorialize the victory it brought you. Go to Gilgal by faith and confess to God every stigma or hint of reproach you feel you've worn. Let Him cut that old piece of fabric from your life, roll it (*galal*) in the blood of Jesus, and cast it away forever.

"The one who calls you is faithful and he will do it" (1 Thess. 5:24).

"March around the city once
with all the armed men.
Do this for six days . . .
On the seventh day, march around
the city seven times. . . ."

Joshua 6:3–4

Chapter Fourteen

Believing God When
Routine Follows Revelation

I hope we're leaving Gilgal with a lighter wardrobe than we wore there. It's high time some of us traded a spirit of heaviness for a garment of praise. Our next stop in the Promised Land is a perch near Jericho where Joshua had an unexpected encounter with the commander of the LORD's army.

"Now when Joshua was near Jericho, he looked up and saw a man standing in front of him with a drawn sword in his hand. Joshua went up to him and asked 'Are you for us or for our enemies?'

(Translation: "Whose side are you on?")

" 'Neither,' he replied, 'but as commander of the army of the LORD I have now come.'

(Translation: "I'm not here to take sides. I'm here to take over.")

"Then Joshua fell facedown to the ground in reverence, and asked him, 'What message does my Lord have for his servant?'

"The commander of the LORD's army replied, 'Take off your sandals, for the place where you are standing is holy.' And Joshua did so" (Josh. 5:13–15).

God is good for His Word. Do you remember back in Joshua 1:9 when God told Joshua to be "strong and courageous"? In the same verse He told His servant why: "For the LORD your God will be with you wherever you go." God promises to always be with us, but every now and then He reveals His presence a little more vividly than we were expecting. That's what God did with Joshua just outside of Jericho. God determined that if His servant was going to step into a holy moment, he'd better do it with bare feet. "And Joshua did so." If I could get a clue about the greatness of God, I'd be mortified by all the times He told me to do something and the record showed, "And Beth did not do so." Help me, Lord.

Many scholars believe the commander of

the LORD's army was a theophany (a manifestation of God) or even a preincarnate appearance of Christ. The title "LORD of Hosts" used elsewhere depicts a similar position of headship over an army (ordinarily angelic), and it is attributed solely to the divine. At first glance, the question of identity seems to be answered in Joshua's reference to the commander as "Lord" in verse 14.

"What message does my Lord have for his servant?"

Note that only the first letter is capitalized in this title (Lord) as opposed to the capitalization of all the letters (LORD) that appear in every other reference to Lordship in this text. When the first letter alone is capitalized, the original Hebrew transliteration is ordinarily *adon* or *adonai*. These forms of the same Hebrew term are often used for God in the Old Testament, but they can also refer to a superior or master of any kind. On the other hand, when the name appears in all capital or small capital letters, it is a covenantal reference (YHWH) for God alone. The most dependable clue the text offers for a theophany is the figure's authority to sanctify the very ground on which they stood and deem it holy. The wording "Take off your sandals, for the place where you are standing is holy" is nearly identical to the command God gave Moses at the burning bush in Exodus 3:5. There the text removes all doubt that the voice was God Himself.

God had promised to be with Joshua wherever he went, and as His servant stood on the cusp of Canaan's summit city, I suppose God thought Joshua could use a fresh revelation. We can well imagine that Joshua's eyebrows were pinned to his hairline and his chin was hanging to the ground. I'm surprised he had to be told to take off his sandals. How they didn't shake off is beyond me.

I'm no Joshua, nor have I seen a manifestation of God Himself, but He has nearly scared the life out of me a few times to let me know He was present. One occasion is particularly fresh on my mind. A few weekends ago I once again got to be part of a huge gathering of college students called OneDay, headed by Louie Giglio of Passion Conferences. Students come from campuses all over the United States and abroad to spend an entire day in solemn assembly to fast and pray and seek God's face. A large piece of land has to be chosen that can support thirty thousand plus college students, their cars, and their camping gear. A platform and stage, complete with lights, giant speakers, and screens is set up for the central gathering place.

I've never experienced anything quite like OneDay. I've long tried to discern the difference, and I think I may have figured it out. Virtually all conferences I'm invited to attend are born of pure hearts and built on serious intentions of meeting with God. OneDay, however, is set apart in the professed willingness of staff and participants to meet with God on His terms rather than asking Him to meet on ours. The staff goes to greater lengths than I've ever seen to make sure spiritual preparations are made far in advance. The students at this last gathering received a CD in the mail with instructions to listen to it in their cars as they drove to the gathering. The recordings on the CD led them in prayer, confessions, contemplations, and praises. In addition, the OneDay staff asks no small sacrifice (prayer, fasting, time, energy, hard work, difficult conditions, etc.) of their volunteers, leaders, and even attendees.

They're into serious stuff. I share this background with you because God ended up doing some serious stuff of His own. Stuff that nearly scared us to death. Since that time I've thought about how often I ask God to reveal Himself mightily and work dramatically. Now I've begun to wonder what we'd do if He really "showed up." I'll tell you about our little glimpse.

The leadership and volunteers had been instructed to be on the grounds by Saturday afternoon, and the students were expected in full on Sunday night. The actual solemn assembly was scheduled for all day Monday. While the main staff moved into assigned RVs on the grounds, hundreds of the volunteers set up tents. About seven thousand students arrived early and set up their tents as well. The sight of all the brightly colored canvas and anxious faces was remarkable. We prayed and prayed for God to come and meet with us, and our hearts were filled with anticipation. Night began to fall, then all of the sudden a storm came. Not just any storm. Thunder was crashing, and lightening was flashing in a heavenly display unlike anything I've experienced in a long time. The sky fell with pounding rain.

I lay in the bed of the RV bug-eyed while it rocked to the rhythm of the storm. I knew nothing else to do but cry out to God. Often all I could say was, "Oh, God, help! Oh, God, have mercy!" I was worried sick for the early arrivals in the tents. I had many loved ones among them, but I was deeply anxious for everyone out there. The storm was the life-threatening kind, and it rocked our world almost all night. If you could have experienced it with us, you'd know what a miracle of God it was that no one was killed.

At the risk of sounding mystical, midway through the night I suddenly began to receive what I believe may have been a revelation of sorts: an unusual spiritual insight that I felt I could trust because it came to me totally through God's Word. All of a sudden Scriptures started coming to my mind that included words like "storm," "thunder," and "lightening" — almost like a concordance was rolling like a scroll through my memory. These are two in particular:

> His way is in the whirlwind and the storm. (Nah. 1:3)

> From the throne came flashes of lightning, rumblings and peals of thunder. (Rev. 4:5)

The fear of God fell upon me in a way that has happened few times in my life. I felt He was saying something like this to all of us: "You asked me to come. You told me you were serious about meeting with Me.

The real Me. And I just thought I'd let you know that I have accepted your invitation. I am arriving."

Those last three words echoed over and over in my mind: "I am arriving."

With fireworks, I might add.

My heart nearly pounded out of my chest. The words of Job 37:1–4 describe in full what I felt in part:

> "At this my heart pounds
> and leaps from its place.
> Listen! Listen to the roar of his voice,
> to the rumbling that comes from
>   his mouth.
> He unleashed his lightning beneath
>   the whole heaven
> and sends it to the ends of the earth.
> After that comes the sound of his
>   roar;
> he thunders with his majestic voice.
> When his voice resounds,
> he holds nothing back."

God wants us to seek Him
and find Him.

I'm not ready to say God held "nothing back" that weekend, but He certainly convinced me that it is only "because of the LORD's great love we are not consumed"

(Lam. 3:22). If not for God's compassion, His very presence in our midst would kill us. We really have little clue who we're dealing with. The good news is: God wants us to seek Him and find Him. He wants to draw us close and find security in Him. He also wants us to appreciate the greatness and majesty of who He is and the gift of the cross to grant us bold access. "The fear of the LORD is the beginning of knowledge" (Prov. 1:7).

I've been in plenty of storms, but I have never been more convinced one had spiritual implications. As it turned out, God did indeed meet with us. We had more than a little revival. We had results. The God kind. Many can't be calculated, but among those that can were eight thousand college students who signed on a dotted line as volunteers for short- and long-term global missions. We cried out to God, and as Job 38:1 says, "The LORD answered [us] out of the storm."

Skeptics might reason that the storm was simply in the forecast. I would argue that a similar storm was also forecast for the next night, yet as if God were making a point, we met for our opening worship service under clear skies and twinkling stars. Rain or shine, the forecast that weekend was God.

I've thought a lot about those students since they returned to their usual surroundings. We saw God work in such gale force that I've wondered if some were let down when the dramatics subsided. Sure, many signed up for missions, and countless others dedicated their lives to follow hard after God, but He may not mobilize them in obvious areas of ministry for years. Many of them now feel chosen and called, just as every other believer in Christ should feel, yet what are they to do until God plants them actively in the land of their harvest?

The day-in day-out fundamentals. That's what.

Go back to the story of Joshua and Jericho with me. You'd think after a dramatic encounter with the commander of the LORD's army Joshua could expect an equally dramatic game plan for Jericho's inevitable fall. That's not exactly what he got. Read the instructions for yourself:

> March around the city once with all the armed men. Do this for six days. Have seven priests carry trumpets of rams' horns in front of the ark. On the seventh day, march around the city seven times, with the priests blowing the trumpets.

When you hear them sound a long blast on the trumpets, have all the people give a loud shout; then the wall of the city will collapse and the people will go up, every man straight in. (Josh. 6:3–5)

If Joshua allowed himself a little human reasoning, I might imagine him thinking something like this: *Can't we just cut to the chase? Why march around the city for six days, then seven more times on the seventh day? What's all this repetition about? Can we just shout on day one and see the walls collapse?*

Surely we don't think the plan made perfect sense to the Israelites, let alone a man like Joshua, whose specialty was war strategy (Exod. 17:13). What good could walking repetitiously around a city accomplish? On that seventh day and about the fourth time around, don't you imagine the same old scenery and the same old pace was getting a little old? What on earth was God doing, and why this way?

I'm not much for numerology, but the repetition of some numbers and their similar contexts can hardly be denied. In Scripture seven is believed by many scholars to be the number of completion. The creation account seems to be the paradigm. The seven days and seven repetitions God required of the Israelites before He'd give them Jericho was a literal time frame for them, but it presents a figurative application for us. Sometimes God requires us to follow a fair amount of repetition for a considerable amount of time until He deems a season complete. Then all of the sudden He seems to do something profound or miraculous, and we can't figure out what changed.

In Scripture seven is believed
by many scholars to be
in the number of completion.

In just a few chapters this book will draw to a close. One of its important messages is that you can still believe God for something dramatic and something miraculous. But in between dramatic revelations, what's a believer to do? The day-in, day-out fundamentals, that's what.

Prayer. A daily time in God's Word. Praise and worship. Attending church. Serving a church body. Giving. These are the fundamentals, and they'll never change. We can make all the excuses in the world for not practicing this one or that, but they represent the backbone of obedience. We often want the mystical while God often insists on the practical. We may want a constant dose of dramatics, but God enjoys seeing the perseverance and proven faithfulness of simple daily devotion. Sometimes the greatest proof of God's miraculous power is when an attention-deficit seeker of instant-gratification denies himself, takes up his cross, and follows Christ . . . for the long haul.

Glance back at your time line for a moment. Our favorite parts are the stones of remembrance strewn here and there on our life path. God's favorite parts are the lines in between where we chose to walk faithfully without answers and visible evidences. I tend to think that our patient faithfulness to walk between dramatic revelations fans the flame of God's desire to show us His glory. In other words, faithfulness invests in the future.

Sometimes we lay a crucial request before God, perhaps a life-and-death matter, and we want something fast and spectacular. Instead, God often directs us to keep walking around that Jericho day after day, repeating the same old fundamental steps while nothing seems to happen. Oh, it will. We must never stop believing it will. But in the meantime, we've got to keep walking and keep circling no matter how many times we've done it before and no matter how many times we're yet to do it.

G. K. Chesterton wrote of a God who "is strong enough to exult in monotony. It is possible that God says every morning, 'Do it again' to the sun; and every evening, 'Do it again' to the moon. It may not be automatic necessity that makes all daisies alike; it may be that God makes every daisy separately, but has never got tired of making them. It may be that He has the eternal appetite of infancy; for we have sinned and grown old."[10]

Ours is a God who delights in a perfect concoction of creativity and order. Though He could have thought the entire cosmos into existence in a millisecond, instead He brought it about with great patience in six distinct increments.

Then rested on the seventh.

Then later insisted that His children do the same.

God likes order. He likes repetition. A God of fundamentals, He brings up the sun every morning and the moon every evening, but His creativity within order is gorgeously displayed in the changing sunsets and sunrises surrounding them. The same is true for us. Faithfulness in our Christian walk requires order, some black-and-white fundamentals, but within that order is glorious room for color and creativity.

I have lived too much of my life in defeat to risk living in the gray zone. A long time ago I had to quit giving myself the option of whether or not to rise for prayer, spend time in the Word that day, or attend and serve my church consistently. These fundamentals are part of my life. They are His will, and to do otherwise — no matter how I'd label it — is disobedience.

Within those fundamentals God gives me lots of leash to exercise my need for passion and drama. Though my morning almost always begins at the same table and chair, it might end out in the yard under the morning stars or, better yet, on a walk. On a rare Saturday at home, I may have my prayer time still tucked in my soft bed. Other times the beach is the perfect place. I take that back. Keep the beach and give me mountains. My point is: I get up daily with the morning, but the sunrise surrounding my time with God could be any number of colors. Sometimes I jump up and down; sometimes I bow down, and sometimes I go prostrate to the ground. Sometimes I pray Scripture. Other times I pray moans and groans. But pray, I must. It's God's will even when I can't tell if it's changing a thing.

Faithfulness in our Christian walk requires order, some black-and-white fundamentals, but within that order is glorious room for color and creativity.

Though I may practice these disciplines in various ways, I do them virtually every day. Why? Because God seems to like them. Picture God nudging you and me awake before dawn because He can hardly wait to be with us. Then as we make our sleepy way to the usual meeting place, imagine Him saying something rather like Chesterton suggested. "Do it again, Child!"

Sometimes I feel like the phrases I habitually use in prayer and the topics I'm most burdened to teach are surely getting old to God. In reality, as long as He sees a genuine heart, He never gets tired of some of the same old words and practices that flow from it. "Say it again, Child! One more time!" God's mercies have existed through all of eternity, yet Scripture tells us they are new every morning. You see, a new day with all its fresh challenges gives an old practice new life.

Day-in and day-out, the fundamentals are the way I march repeatedly around my Jerichos. Unlike Joshua and the Israelites, I never know when my present Jericho is going to fall. I just know that I'm to keep believing and keep marching. When the time is complete, the wall is going to collapse. When the Israelites marched around Jericho, their seventh trip around on the seventh day could not have seemed any different from the rest, with the exception that they were wearier. Why did God purpose for the wall to fall on that particular round? Simply because it was time.

Beloved, God is not tired. Nor is God tired of you. He delights in your attentions even when you practice them much like you did yesterday. He waits for you to awaken, and he anticipates His time with you. When you or I ignore Him, He is disappointed. Somehow in His self-existent essence and omniscience, His foreknowledge does not cheat Him of reactive emotion. He laughs when you delight Him. He listens when you speak to Him. He honors you when you persevere with Him. In all the changes He is making within you and me, He rejoices in the few things that call for blessed sameness.

Let's stay faithful, you and I. "Let us not

become weary in doing good, for at the proper time we will reap a harvest if we do not give up" (Gal. 6:9).

"There has never been a day like
it before or since, . . ."

Joshua 10:14

Chapter Fifteen

Believing God When Victory Demands Your All

On the other hand, sometimes life has more excitement than we can bear, and nothing about today vaguely resembles yesterday. This chapter is a purposeful follow-up to the last. Chapter 14 dealt with seasons that may begin with fireworks but settle into the day-in, day-out fundamentals of a steady faith walk. Essentially the message was persevering in seasons of sameness. This chapter, on the other hand, is about times when we get change we don't want for reasons we don't like and we'd give anything for life to go back to a daily routine. Meet me in the tenth chapter of the book of Joshua.

Now Adoni-Zedek king of Jerusalem heard that Joshua had taken Ai and totally destroyed it, doing to Ai and its king as he had done to Jericho and its king, and that the people of Gibeon had made a treaty of peace with Israel and were living near them. He and his people were very much alarmed at this, because Gibeon was an important city, like one of the royal cities; it was larger than Ai, and all its men were good fighters. So Adoni-Zedek king of Jerusalem appealed to Hoham king of Hebron, Piram king of Jarmuth, Japhia king of Lachish and Debir king of Eglon. "Come up and help me attack Gibeon," he said, "because it has made peace with Joshua and the Israelites."

Then the five kings of the Amorites — the kings of Jerusalem, Hebron, Jarmuth, Lachish and Eglon — joined forces. They moved up with all their troops and took up positions against Gibeon and attacked it.

The Gibeonites then sent word to Joshua in the camp at Gilgal: "Do not abandon your servants. Come up to us quickly and save us! Help us, because all the Amorite kings from the hill country have joined forces against us."

So Joshua marched up from Gilgal with his entire army, including all the best fighting men. The LORD said to Joshua, "Do not be afraid of them; I have given them into your hand. Not one of them will be able to withstand you."

After an all-night march from Gilgal, Joshua took them by surprise. The LORD threw them into confusion before Israel, who defeated them in a great victory at Gibeon. Israel pursued them along the road going up to Beth Horon and cut them down all the way to Azekah and Makkedah. As they fled before Israel on the road down from Beth Horon to Azekah, the LORD hurled large hailstones down on them from the sky, and more of them died from the hailstones than were killed by the swords of the Israelites.

On the day the LORD gave the Amorites over to Israel, Joshua said to the LORD in the presence of Israel:

"O sun, stand still over Gibeon,
O moon, over the Valley of Aijalon."

So the sun stood still,
and the moon stopped,
till the nation avenged itself on
its enemies,
    as it is written in the Book of
Jashar.

The sun stopped in the middle of the sky and delayed going down about a full day. There has never been a day like it before or since, a day when the LORD listened to a man. Surely the LORD was fighting for Israel! (Josh. 10:1–14)

If you've walked with God for many years, you've probably noticed that what He requires from us to live in victory can differ greatly from season to season. Consider a few common scenarios:

- Sometimes in our challenges, He directs us to simply "Be still, and know that [He] is God" (Ps. 46:10). In other words, "Keep up your day-in, day-out fundamentals, be still in me, and trust that I am in total control. I don't want your involvement on this issue. I just want you to practice keeping your hands off of it and letting me have it."
- Other times He seems to command us to "stand firm and you will see the deliverance the LORD will bring you

today . . . the LORD will fight for you" (Exod. 14:13–14). In other words, "Retain your stillness in knowing that I am God but in an upright posture of watchfulness." I sense a greater alertness in this directive, much like Ephesians 6:13 that tells us to put on the "whole armor of God" and "having done all, to stand."

- Still other times we may sense God saying, "Let me see you wield the sword of the Spirit and use your weapons of warfare." Of course, we are called to be in God's Word consistently, but we don't always have a sense of active satanic opposition. In this category God calls the reserve into heightened active duty to "demolish arguments and every pretension that sets itself up against the knowledge of God" (2 Cor. 10:5). When commissioned by God to active participation in the fight, if we just stand and watch as we did in another season, we'll nearly get slaughtered by the evil one.
- Then again, seasons exist like the one we're going to study in this chapter, times when God demands everything we've got. He seems to say, "I've got a great victory in store for you, but if you want it, you'll have to give Me nothing less than your all. I want 100 percent.

This season will take every bit of the focus you've got, and you will literally live on My strength to get through it." Like the previous example, this season involves warfare, but this time the heat doesn't let up. This time you feel as if your life, or someone else's, depends on it. In times like these, we can't even think about tomorrow because we don't know how on earth we're going to live through the battle today.

When victory demands our all. That's what this message is all about. Calculate a few elements that made the battle in Joshua 10 applicable.

Consider the physical challenges. The odds were five to one: one army of Israelites to five armies of Canaanites. The Israelites had to step out in faith and commit to the battle before they received any word from God concerning the outcome (v. 7). Their humiliating loss at Ai (Josh. 7), fresh on their minds, evaporated the luxury of thinking a battle fought was a battle won. Scripture tells us they had an all-night march, and geography tells us they had an uphill battle, a four-thousand-foot ascent of rugged terrain without the benefit of rest.

Thankfully, somewhere in the process

Joshua received a word from God that He was going to give them the victory, but don't think for a moment the Israelites could stand back and watch. This wasn't a "be still" moment. Nor was it a "stand still" moment. Certainly it was a "wield your sword" moment, but the relentless demand throws it into the fourth category. This was a "100 percent/all you've got" moment. God gave them an awesome victory, but I'd like to suggest that He required every ounce of energy and cooperation they had in the process. Joshua didn't ask for the sun to stand still for nothing. He needed the sun to stay put in the sky because the time was growing slim and the enemy was not yet conquered.

God could have given over the enemy quickly or dropped them dead in their tracks at the end of the day. Instead, He allowed Joshua to discern that he was going to need more time (v. 13). So, you see, God gave the Israelites the battle, but He required their participation to the tune of no sleep, an all-night march uphill, and a day of fierce battle only to see that the enemy was not yet down. The darkness would have been a serious strike against them in an unfamiliar land; hence, Joshua's prayer.

As tempted as we may be to romanticize scenes like this, in reality the winners drenched that battlefield in sweat and received the victory with serious body odor. I'd like to suggest that some of the most adventurous endeavors you'll have with God may be too difficult at the time to enjoy, and by the time the party comes, you may smell too bad to go. Ah, but after a shower and a good look back! We'll get to that later.

As if the physical challenges weren't enough, *consider the psychological challenges.* If you read the account closely, you caught the fact that the Gibeonites involved Joshua and the Israelites in this battle. The background of their association is key to grasping the mental hardship of the battle. In Joshua 9, we find that the Gibeonites deceived the Israelites into making a peace treaty with them. God's people had been forbidden to enter covenants with the nearby Canaanite peoples, so the Gibeonites masqueraded themselves and their provisions to appear as if they had come from afar. Because everything looked legitimate, the Israelites did not bother inquiring of the LORD (9:14). Instead, they proceeded with the treaty. Interestingly, the Israelites failed to inquire of the Lord, but they didn't fail to invoke His name when they swore a hasty oath to the Gibeonites (9:18). In doing so, they bound themselves permanently.

Just think about all the opportunities the Israelites had to lose this battle psychologically. They could have been preoccupied with at least three negatives:

- *How unfair it was.* I wonder if you've ever fought a fiercely demanding battle you didn't cause. An illness? A layoff? The untimely death of a loved one? A house fire? Suddenly worthless stocks? Any number of situations can arise that you or I didn't cause, yet we're thrown into long-term overdrive to deal with them. Some of the most difficult and demanding seasons of our lives will seem grossly unfair. We can expend so much energy whining about the unfairness of our situation that we have nothing left to invest in the real fight.

- *Whose fault it was.* This psychological challenge goes a step further than unfairness because it offers the element of blame. Have you ever ended up fighting the battle of your life that somebody else dragged you into? Did a spouse walk out and leave you to raise three difficult teenagers . . . who, incidentally, decided to blame you instead of your spouse? Did a business partner make a decision that virtually bankrupted the company? Did a parent die refusing to resolve conflict with you? Were you hit by a drunk driver and left with physical handicaps? Or, like the Israelites, did someone deceive you into some kind of involvement that had terrifying consequences? Did someone you trusted betray you and leave you in a terrible mess? As the Israelites trudged that steep terrain with no sleep and fought until their hands could have frozen to the sword, don't you think the thought occurred to them, "The Gibeonites tricked us. This battle is their fault. They ought to get what they have coming to them!" Few things compete mentally with the blame game.

Not only could the Israelites have become preoccupied about how unfair it was and whose fault it was, they could also have glanced at their own reflection in the nearest pond and thought . . .

- *How stupid they were.* Oh, this one's huge. Don't you think the Israelites could have kicked themselves from Gilgal to the Dead Sea for their lack of discernment and failure to inquire of the Lord? Haven't you and I been there?

What happens when you've got some-one to blame and that someone is you? I remember finding myself in the biggest mess of my adult life because I talked myself out of a nagging feeling that a certain situation was beyond me. As clearly as yesterday, I remember hitting myself (hard) on the head as I sobbed, "You are so stupid! How could you be so stupid?" I have a funny friend who says, "Sin can be forgiven, but stupid is forever." That's how it feels sometimes. I unfortunately dealt with a double por-tion of sinfulness and stupidity.

All of these mind-sets are written invita-tions to bitterness engraved on hardening hearts. How often do we lose the battle to our own bitterness rather than to our op-position? Make no mistake: Satan's spe-cialty is psychological warfare. If he can turn us on God ("It's not fair!"), turn us on others ("It's their fault!"), or turn us on ourselves ("I'm so stupid!"), we won't turn on him. If we keep fighting within our-selves and losing our own inner battles, we'll never have the strength to stand up and fight our true enemy.

Joshua 10:10 tells us that God enabled Israel to defeat all five kingdoms "in a great victory at Gibeon." The Hebrew word for "great victory" translates best in English as "a great wounding." Dear One, God doesn't just want us to defend ourselves in fierce seasons of battle. He wants us to wound the kingdom of darkness. Satan knows that "greater is he that is in you, than he that is in the world" (1 John 4:4 KJV). He just hopes you don't know it.

Keith and I adopted a saying many years ago when we were watching one of the early *Rocky* sequels. We stared at the screen while Apollo Creed pummeled Rocky's poor face without getting a single return punch. Keith leaned over me and said, "That's the old 'let 'em hit you in the face 'til they're tired' trick." We've labeled many situations by that old trick since then. Some of us think that if we just stand there and let Satan hit us long enough, he'll get tired. He's not getting tired! Hit him back, for crying out loud!

We've got a battle to fight, and God wants us to dent the very gates of hell. Fighting the good fight of faith takes energy! So do self-pity, anger, unforgiveness, and self-loathing. Each of us must decide where we're going to put our energy when the battle grows fierce.

God alone can give us the daily dose of grace not to grow bitter in a long-term battle (Heb. 12:15). Satan will do everything he can to try to keep us from receiving the grace God extends. One of his primary approaches is trying to convince us that God withholds His help *after the fact* if we didn't ask for His help *before the fact*. He wants us to believe that God is sitting on His throne huffing, "You got yourself into this mess; now get yourself out." Beloved, I want to assure you that some of the most awesome things God has ever done for me have come out of the most awful things I'd done to myself.

Whether the circumstances that lead to our fiercest battles are someone else's fault, our own fault, or the fruit of life's unfairness, having God as our Father grants us this hope: A perfect setup for catastrophic defeat is also the perfect setup for miraculous victory. No matter how we got into a mess, we just have to keeping believing that . . .

God is who He says He is.
God can do what He says He can do.
I am who God says I am.
I can do all things through Christ.
God's Word is alive and active in me.

Those who decide to be preoccupied with believing God over their own negative emotions will sooner or later discover what Joshua did:

God loves big prayers! What in the world came over Joshua to make him ask for time to freeze? How did the thought even occur to him? And, for heaven's sake, why did he take the chance of looking foolish by asking for it "in the presence of Israel" (Josh. 10:12)? Had I been him and suddenly gotten the notion to ask, I would have engaged God in a quick game of charades.

I am astonished by Joshua's boldness to ask for something that had literally never happened before. God later interrupted time for Hezekiah, but Joshua had never heard of such a thing. He just knew God could and reasoned that he might as well ask Him if He would. Joshua had that Jeremiah 32:17 mentality:

Ah, Sovereign LORD, you have made the heavens and the earth by your great power and outstretched arm. Nothing is too hard for you.

You and I could use the same mentality. Maybe we could catch it from Joshua since I'm pretty sure he caught it from Moses. Do you remember the time God caused "all [His] goodness to pass in front of" Moses and hid him nearby in the cleft of a rock while He passed by Him with His glory? (Exod. 33:19–23). Moses' encounter with God in that scene is unmatched in Scripture. Why did Moses get to experience such a thing? Maybe because he had guts enough to ask. He placed His request before God with the words, "Now show me your glory" (Exod. 33:18).

God glories in big prayers from people with a big God. Not a big ego. If, like Moses, our chief desire is for God to show His glory, God may delight in giving us our own special glimpse in the process. Joshua also set his sights on God's glory. He understood that the point of all victory in the Promised Land was the fame of one true God before the polytheistic Canaanites. After the disaster of Ai and the prospect of defeat, he asked God, "What then will you do for your own great name?" (Josh. 7:9). In Joshua 10, as he led the army of Israel against five kingdoms, he knew that God was going to give the enemy into their hands for His name's sake; therefore, as daylight burned and the enemy still stood, he had guts enough to ask God for a staggering miracle to accomplish His will. You need to know and count on the fact that God is willing to interrupt the very laws of nature to perform His will.

While we're at it, never underestimate the place of humility in the power of prayer. My man is the most unpretentious person I've ever met, which is precisely why he felt chosen by God in our early years to call out any pretense he saw in me. He's never been big on himself, but his God is pretty big. Keith has struggled a lot with consistency along the way, and I'm fairly certain he'd consider himself to be the least spiritual, and the least faithful, in our family. I assure you, that's not true, but, as I said, he's never been big on himself.

Yesterday morning the skies suddenly dumped a ton of water on our part of Houston. In a matter of minutes, the water dripped through our ceiling and rose within an inch of our back door. The sound of it on our roof was nearly deafening. In a state of near panic, I grabbed Keith by the arm and pulled him to the back door. He opened it up, gazed at the water for a moment, then lifted up his right arm and said, "Stretch forth Your mighty hand, O God, and recede the waters." Instantly (I don't mean a few seconds later), the roar ceased, the torrent turned into a few final sprinkles, and the rain stopped. (Where was Keith that scary night at OneDay?) I stood slack jawed. He turned around and looked at me with such a shocked expression that I laugh out loud every time I think of it. I also happen to think God got a good knee slapper out of it. A few hours later I answered the phone at work, and my husband muttered, "Was that spooky, or what?"

Beloved, stop looking at others as more spiritual than you and just start believing God!

I am convinced that if I had asked the same thing, God probably wouldn't have done it . . . or at least not so dramatically. I have seen many displays of miraculous intervention over the last six years, and though I would have been blessed and convenienced by God stopping the rain, my faith didn't need the jolt right then. Keith's did. My man needs to know that God is as willing to work in his life and his surroundings as his wife's, and lately God has been going out of His way to show him. Beloved, stop looking at others as more spiritual than you and just start believing God! God's not looking for spiritual "giants." They have a strange way of blocking the layperson's view of God. God is looking for believers who believe for a change.

Let me throw in a disclaimer here before we proceed to the next point. God can delight in our courage to pray big prayers without necessarily giving us what we ask. Let me say that again another way: God can say yes to the heart of our prayer without saying yes to the request of our prayer. God always honors big prayer coming from a small ego with a big God. He will approve of the petitioner even when, for whatever reason, He can't approve the petition. As I stated much earlier in this book, I believe faith always pleases God (Heb. 11:6) even if it prompts an off-target petition. I'm convinced God is more pleased when we believe Him enough to ask for a hundred huge things, though they be granted in part, than to believe Him for a few and get everything we asked. We all err in many ways. Let me err on the side of faith.

Not only will we discover with Joshua that God loves big prayers, we'll discover that *when God requires 100 percent, He might return a hundredfold.* Perhaps you've been waiting for us to get to the part of Joshua's story when God dropped such huge hailstones from the sky that they killed more Canaanites than the swords of the Israelites. Can you picture Joshua calling Caleb later on his cell phone and saying, "Was that spooky, or what?"

I don't think we see a time in the Promised Land when God required more sweat and strain out of Joshua and the Israelites than He did in Joshua 10. Not coincidentally, they never again saw such miraculous intervention.

Hailstones from heaven.

The stop of a clock.

Huge works of God! Joshua 10:14 says, "There has never been a day like it before or since." Dear One, when God requires much, He'll do even more. God is faithful. You will never invest more in Him than He will in you. God's Word tells us to whom much is given, much is required (Luke 12:48), but I am also convinced that to whom much is required, much is surely given.

Sooner or later.

One way or the other.

A mansion for a mustard seed.

A kingdom for a pauper.

This you can take to the spiritual bank: Life is not fair. And there *is* someone to blame: Jesus Christ. "From the fullness of his grace we have all received one blessing after another" (John 1:16). And wouldn't I be stupid to miss that?

One last thing when victory demands your all. Sometimes God requires so much of us just so we can experience the un-matched exhilaration of partnering in divine triumph. As badly as they smelled at the end of the battle, can you imagine a single Israelite in Joshua's army saying, "I'd just as soon have stayed home. I may never get the stains out of this robe or the broken strap fixed on this sandal." No way! They talked about this battle on their deathbeds! Their grandchildren sat spell-bound as they recounted every detail: the masquerading Gideonites, the foolish treaty, the cry for help when they should have owed them nothing, the all-night march, the uphill battle, the hailstones on steroids, the sun stuck over Gibeon, and the moon stuck over the Valley of Aijalon. There had never been a day like it. And they wouldn't have missed it for the world.

God can say yes to the heart of our prayer without saying yes to the request of our prayer.

God has so much for you, Dear One.

And, yes, seasons will come when He requires so much from you that you feel like you can't bear it. You do have a choice. You don't have to do it His way. You can choose bitterness, resentment, carnality, or mediocrity. Or you can go for it. With everything you've got. You can experience the unmatched exhilaration of partnering in divine triumph. The stakes are high. The cost is steep. But I'll promise you this: there is no high like the Most High.

Don't miss it for the world.

"Clap your hands, all you nations; shout to God with cries of joy. How awesome is the LORD Most High, the great King over all the earth!" (Ps. 47:1–2).

"The only thing that counts is faith expressing itself through love."

Galatians 5:6

Chapter Sixteen

Believing God for Love

Knowing our time together is drawing quickly to a close, I feel somewhat like I did when I left my firstborn at college and scrambled to say some final paramount things. God placed such a high priority on believing Him that prioritizing some faith practices over others seems impossible. Under the inspiration of the Holy Spirit, one faith practice floated to the top for the apostle Paul. He wrote, "The only thing that counts is faith expressing itself through love" (Gal. 5:6).

Early on in our journey we discussed that faith is God's favorite invitation to make the impossible possible. He is greatly glorified when we are each enabled to do what we're unable to do. I can think of few things further beyond our capabilities than loving those we don't want to love and loving those we don't even like.

If we place 2 Corinthians 5:7 (which

tells us to live by faith and not by sight) next to Galatians 5:6, I believe we can come up with two life challenges that, if accepted, catapult us onto a path infinitely higher than this world's self-centered interstate of mediocrity:

We live by faith. We love by faith.

Though the call to love is issued repeatedly throughout the New Testament, Ephesians 5:1–2 presents it best as a lifestyle:

> Be imitators of God, therefore, as dearly loved children and live a life of love, just as Christ loved us and gave himself up for us as a fragrant offering and sacrifice to God.

The One who adopted us into His royal family has called us to live according to our legacy. We are to literally *live love.* Fuzzy thought, isn't it? But check the verse again. The very nature of love is sacrificial. In fact, if we're not presently feeling the squeeze and sacrifice of loving, we're probably exercising a preferential, highly selective, self-centered human substitute.

Not only have we been called to live a sacrificial love, in certain situations we may expend untold self-sacrificing efforts *for years,* if not for the rest of our lives, without seeing any apparent fruit. God has

called us to love even when . . .
- We don't want to.
- We don't feel like it.
- We get nothing obvious in return.
- They don't deserve it.
- They're not worth it.
- They don't even know it.
- It makes no difference.

If we're not confronted by God to love someone in this season of our lives who brings out many of those feelings in us, we're probably not getting out enough. Mind you, loving sacrificially does *not* equal subjecting ourselves to untold abuses. God doesn't call us to sacrifice our sanity; He calls us to sacrifice our selfishness. When those lines are unclear, I can give you no more important advice than to seek sound, godly counsel, just as I have done.

We live by faith.
We love by faith.

You might be relieved to know that we can love without feeling all warm and fuzzy. One of the distinctive dimensions of *agape*, the Greek word most commonly translated "love" in the New Testament, is the active participation of volition or will.

In other words, *agape* is not only exercised when it feels like it, it is exercised when we choose to extend God's love as an (often sacrificial) act of our will. Sometimes our only motivation is obedience to God. When we're willing, we're succinctly told in 1 Corinthians 13:8 that *love never fails.*

A lump wells in my throat as I stare at those three words because for years I wanted to argue, "Yes it does! At least mine does!" As poor and misguided as my attempts were at times, I tried my hardest to love a certain little boy to wholeness for seven years, and I felt I failed. That's because I didn't understand what the promise meant. I thought it meant that love wouldn't fail to bring about the exact results I wanted and had asked for. The word *fail* actually portrays something that drops or falls to the ground, thereby having no effect. With a better grasp on the concept these days, I can make you a bold biblical promise: Beloved, when you really love, difficultly and sacrificially, God catches it even if no one else does. It never falls to the ground.

Never. Not once. Not ever. According to the Book of Truth, we are incapable of loving in Jesus' name and for the sake of His sacrificial legacy for nothing. Love absolutely cannot fail. Each of us has to decide whether we're going to believe God's Word or we're going to believe our eyes and our own emotions. This is where loving by faith comes in. We've got to know that every effort to love sacrificially never fails . . .

- to get the priority attention of God (Mark 12:28–30).
- to ultimately and undoubtedly be rewarded.
- to have a profound effect, whether in the other person, in the circumstance, or in *us*. (And maybe even in God. Have you ever considered that when He took the chance of loving us, He took the risk of being affected by us?)

The tears still sting in my eyes over not getting the results I wanted from that seven-year, deeply felt exercise of love, but my soul's consolation is knowing none of the work fell to the ground. It's in God's hands. You've got to know that too.

Love by faith. Love our enemies by faith. Love our neighbors by faith. Love fellow believers by faith. Love our family members by faith. Love our spouses by faith. Love our in-laws by faith. Love a rebellious teenager by faith. Love our betrayer by faith. Love an ill and bitter parent by faith.

Love by faith, not just by feeling.

Love is not a spiritual gift. Otherwise we'd all conveniently claim not to possess that particular anointing. Rather, love is a supreme and priority calling: the fruit of the Spirit of Christ within us that surfaces when we are filled by Him, yielded to His authority (Gal. 5:22–23; Eph. 5:18). The chief reason we find loving so painful, aggravating, and fruitless is because we keep trying to love with the pitifully small resources of our own emotional tank. Romans 5:5 is my favorite Scripture to pray when I am challenged to love someone. (This is a Scripture begging for an index card.)

"And hope does not disappoint us, because God has poured out his love into our hearts by the Holy Spirit, whom he has given us." — Romans 5:5

Living *agape* is a daily commitment of the will to vacate the premises of the heart with its own preferential affections, and make its chambers a fleshy canteen for the liquid love of God. Yes, it's still a challenge, but it's no longer the impossible dream. We live by faith. We love by faith. Faith and love are inseparable housemates that offer hospitality to hope. When we lose our faith to love, we lose the energy to love. Then we lose our hope.

Beloved, when all is said and done, living is for loving. So, these three remain: *"faith, hope and love. But the greatest of these is love"* (1 Cor. 13:13). This is our daily hope: faith expressing itself through love. Sometimes it has interesting consequences.

And hope does not disappoint us,
because God has poured out his love
into our hearts by the Holy Spirit,
whom he has given up. — Romans 5:5

I want to warn you about a relational road hazard for those who walk, live, and love by present-active-participle faith. If you truly become a person who makes a lifestyle of believing God, you will become bolder in your love for others and what you're willing to believe God for in their lives. Your fruit is going to start showing, and so is the power of your prayer life. Along the way people around you are liable to start holding you responsible for God's actions. Trust me, I've been there. Scripture has a good name for what some people try to make a person of active faith: false christs. People are so desperate to find Christ that they are willing to manufacture Him out of a mortal with any vague resemblance.

My first brush with what I'll call the False Christ Syndrome happened when I was in college and in a friend's wedding. I was the most spiritual person she knew at that time, which means she didn't get out much. How in the world any witness survived my defeat and hypocrisy is beyond me. Her wedding was scheduled to be outside, and the sky was practically falling with rain. When I arrived and started to make myself comfortable, she took one look at me and growled, "Don't even think of sitting down. Get over there and start praying for that rain to stop!" Boy, did I! God felt sorry for me and stopped the rain, but His unwillingness to rebuke the humidity still left her aghast at our hair. I laugh about it now, but I've since been placed in some positions that weren't nearly as funny.

Loving people means wanting the best for them. Naturally, we often see what is best for others through the limited filter of earthly life. You and I have each experienced times when we've prayed our hardest for several people to be healed of physical illness. One is delivered on earth; the other is delivered in heaven. We've also prayed for people struggling to makes ends meet. One gets a job. Sometimes the other loses her home. Some people reason that God does what He wants and our prayers mean nothing, but the Truth of God's Word differs starkly. The believing prayers of those who pursue a sanctified walk with Jesus Christ are powerful and effectual (James 5:16). So why does God sometimes bring such different results from the same depth of earnest, believing prayer?

- We don't know.
- We're not supposed to know.
- And we're not responsible for the One who does.
- We are not God. We are His children.

As we deeply desire to love and help people, we must be careful not to allow them to make us feel responsible for getting something from God or explaining His mysterious actions. If we do, we are letting them make us false christs, and we have escorted them not only into inevitable disappointment but into God-offending idolatry. Jesus' first followers were surely in these kinds of positions constantly. They lived and loved by faith, but, remember, they didn't get everything they asked for either. I think God reasons that the hearts and minds of mortals can't handle unwavering success even in spiritual terms.

Though they also received no's they couldn't have understood, the disciples continued to live by faith and love by faith for the rest of their days. They relished seeing God do amazing things for others but often added a disclaimer that I think protected them the next time around. After God used Peter and John to heal a crippled beggar at the Gate Beautiful, Peter issued a perfect example of a wise disclaimer:

"Men of Israel, why does this surprise you? Why do you stare at us as if by our own power or godliness we had made this man walk? The God of Abraham, Isaac and Jacob, the God of our fathers, has glorified his servant Jesus" (Acts 3:12).

As we wind down our walk together, we are wise to remind one another never to forget who we are and never to forget who we're not. We're not God. Give up trying. And give up asking anyone else to try. We are to be vessels of His love, not God Himself. Our part is to believe God. His part is to be God and do what is ultimately and eternally best. He alone knows the ultimate objective to which He aligns every divine act on behalf of His children. All are dearly loved. All intricately planned for. God never sits on His hands.

As we actively love others and risk praying big prayers for them, when we receive what we ask, let's not dream of taking credit. When we get to participate in a miracle, let's avoid ever letting another marvel at us or admire us. If we take credit when we receive what we ask, not only will we offend God and mislead people, we will place ourselves in the position to take credit when we don't get what we ask. I am continually reminded of a bumper sticker I once saw: *There is a God. You are not Him.* Glance back at the wording in Acts 3:12 again. None of us possesses enough *power* or *godliness* to enact a miracle in someone else's life on our best day. "Faith expressing itself through love" is a miracle in itself.

By faith, keep living, keep risking, and keep loving. Love others not by trying to become their God but by fueling their faith in God. Work to love and will to love, and when the intended recipient won't catch it, God will.

"Thus far the Lord helped us."

1 Samuel 7:12

Chapter Seventeen

Believing God Ever After

We've come to the place on our path of faith where each of us goes our own way. At my church each week, we bid one another God-speed to our separate walks of faith through a musical benediction. As you and I have made our way through the pages of this faith journey, the notes of one song have danced on the scores of my mind to the voice of the incomparable Rich Mullins. That it should be our benediction is only fitting, so allow me to celebrate the words with you. By the way, in case you're unfamiliar, you don't casually listen to the late Rich Mullins's songs. You analyze them while they analyze you. So take your time here.

I believe in God the Father
Almighty Maker of Heaven
and Maker of Earth
And in Jesus Christ His
only begotten Son, our Lord

He was conceived by the Holy Spirit,
Born of the virgin Mary,
Suffered under Pontius Pilate,
He was crucified and dead and buried.

And I believe what I believe
is what makes me what I am
I did not make it,
no it is making me
It is the very truth of God
and not the invention of any man

I believe that He who suffered
was crucified, buried and dead
He descended into hell
and on the third day,
He rose again
He ascended into Heaven
where He sits at God's mighty right hand
I believe that He's returning
To judge the quick and the dead
of the sons of men

I believe in God the Father
Almighty Maker of Heaven
and Maker of Earth
And in Jesus Christ His
only begotten Son, our Lord
I believe in the Holy Spirit
One Holy Church

The communion of Saints
The forgiveness of sins
I believe in the resurrection,
I believe in a life that never ends

And I believe that what I believe
is what makes me what I am
I did not make it,
no it is making me
It is the very truth of God
and not the invention of any man.[11]

Creed. Rich Mullins knew that God made a man *who he was* but how much that man believed what God said in many ways made him *what he was.* My desire at this moment is to behold the beauty of his words. Oh, that we would not miss it splitting doctrinal hairs over his exact wording. As a people who have taken this journey of fresh belief together, let's sit here and reflect for a moment, gather the meaning to our breast, and nod. We have stated the same concept perhaps a hundred different ways over the last sixteen chapters. Most concisely, *believing God is what closes the gap between our theology and our reality.* Maybe what we believe doesn't so much make us *what* we are as *how* we are. Undoubtedly, how we're doing at any given time in our spiritual walk will depend on who and what we're believing.

I did not make it; no, it is making me.

Long before Rich Mullins was scheduled for arrival on planet Earth, the New Testament church had its own song of Creed. First Timothy 3:16 reads:

> He appeared in a body,
> was vindicated by the Spirit,
> was seen by angels,
> was preached among the nations,
> was believed on in the world,
> was taken up in glory.

Many scholars and traditional commentators through the centuries believe these words were a familiar hymn in the early New Testament church. One indication is the context clarified in the preceding verse. Paul spoke of "God's household, which is the church of the living God, the pillar and foundation of the truth" (1 Tim. 3:15). Picture your earliest brothers and sisters in Christ in their gathering places singing this hymn with passion and conviction, bearing triumphant smiles or sacrificial tears upon their faces. Imagine Peter and John, Mary the mother of Jesus, Mary of Magdala, and all the others harmonizing the creed of their faith. The church was under terrible persecution. They were dying by the dozens for the belief system they hailed in that song. Dozens would turn into hundred and hundreds into thousands. People would die in droves, but no dictator, no matter how powerful, could kill the creed.

Picture the apostle Paul singing those very words with every drop of remaining energy while the wounds of thirty-nine lashes were still wet on his back. I wonder if this hymn happened to be among those he and Silas sang from inside the prison "after they had been severely flogged" (Acts 16:23). Acts 16:25 tells us the other prisoners intently listened to them praying and singing hymns. Paul was such an evangelist that once he knew he had their attention, I wouldn't be at all surprised if he sang them a sound song of biblical doctrine. Whatever they sang, "suddenly there was such a violent earthquake that the foundations of the prison were shaken. At once all the prison doors flew open, and everybody's chains came loose" (Acts 16:26).

God sends His Word forth,
and it never returns void,
unchaining the soul of every person
with the courage to believe it.

Paul believed what Christ believed. It's what made him what he was. He did not make it. No, it was making him. It was the very truth of God and not the invention of any man.

No whip could beat it out of him.

From his last imprisonment the apostle Paul wrote that though he was chained, "God's word is not chained" (2 Tim. 2:9). Indeed it is not. God sends His Word forth, and it never returns void, unchaining the soul of every person with the courage to believe it. Beloved, as we go our separate ways, may we commission one another to spend our lives devouring it. We only have one certain way of knowing that . . .

> **God is who He says He is.**
> **God can do what He says He can do.**
> **I am who God says I am.**
> **I can do all things through Christ.**
> **God's Word is alive and active in me.**

Breathe it. Believe it. Speak it. Live it. Love it. And brace yourself for it.

"The Bible is not a book for the faint of heart — it is a book full of all the greed and glory and violence and tenderness and sex and betrayal that befits mankind. It is not the collection of pretty little anecdotes mouthed by pious little church mice — it does not so much nibble at our shoe leather as it cuts to the heart and splits the marrow from the bone. It does not give us answers fitted to our small-minded questions, but truth that goes beyond what we even know to ask."[12]

Thank you, Dear One, for the joy of your company along this path of faith. I will never forget this adventure as long as I live. I conclude this series with more affection, appreciation, and devotion for the true church of Jesus Christ than I have ever felt before. I have had the privilege of walking this path with people from all sorts of denominations and dimensions of the body of Christ. If you're like me, you desperately needed a little sound biblical permission to take God at His Word. How I pray you've received that, for "without faith it is impossible to please God" (Heb. 11:6).

I'd like to "believe and therefore speak" a few appropriate blessings over you in light of our time lines:

- May your line stay straight and steady.
- May your eyes remain fixed on Jesus, the Author and Finisher of your faith, who awaits you at your finish line.

- And may the path between your today and your eternity be strewn with stones of remembrance.

In just a moment I'm going to ask you to conclude by turning once again to your time line and labeling two final portions of it.

A couple of years ago I sat across a booth from Kay Arthur as we shared breakfast. Amazed at the authority of Christ that rested on her, I finally said, "You have the confidence to know you're going to make it to your finish line victoriously, don't you?" Without hesitation, she responded enthusiastically, "Yes!"

"How do you have such confidence?" I asked.

In typical Kay Arthur fashion, she responded to me with Scripture. "First John 5, that's how! Verses 14 and 15 say, 'This is the confidence which we have before Him, that, if we ask anything according to His will, He hears us. And if we know that He hears us in whatever we ask, we know that we have the requests which we have asked from Him' (NASB). I was tired of living my life in sin. I deeply wanted to live the rest of my days without returning to my old ways. I wept before Him in prayer, pointed to these Scriptures, and asked Him to enable me never to turn back to sin. Because I know it's His will, I know He hears me, and I have what I asked."

Kay put it so simply: "Because I asked Him for it and know it's His will, I know I have it."

Without faith it is impossible to believe God. — Hebrews 11:6

I had also asked God for it. Desperately and with bitter tears and countless pleas. I have a sinful past, and I never want to return to a pit as long as I live. I had asked God countless times to take me to heaven before He let me fall into another pit. The difference between Kay and me was that she believed God the first time.

I've decided to start believing Him for a victorious future too. Don't misunderstand me. I have no intention of thinking I stand, lest I fall (1 Cor. 10:12). With my history I'd be an idiot. Confidence in long-term victory is confidence in God alone. He's given me a visual that has helped me immensely and one that fits beautifully on our time line. After Samuel the prophet led the wayward children of Israel to repentance and wholehearted recommitment, they faced their first battle, and God gave them the victory.

"Then Samuel took a stone and set it up between Mizpah and Shen. He named it Ebenezer, saying, 'Thus far has the LORD helped us'" (1 Sam. 7:12).

Ebenezer means "stone of help." As we walk out the remainder of our time line of faith, let's keep memorializing God's obvious interventions and spiritual markers through stones of remembrance. In the meantime, by faith let's walk with a (figurative) stone in our hand as an "Ebenezer" until we see the next astonishing evidence or spiritual marker and lay it on our line. You see, the "Ebenezer" stone constantly reminds us, "Thus far has the LORD helped us." In other words, with God's help we're making it so far, and we'll make it some more.

I have known the power of addictive sins and strongholds in my life. I know how bleak the prospect of living the next several decades victoriously can be. I remember a time when I couldn't even picture victoriously living the next year, the next month, or the next week, for crying out loud. God spoke to my heart and said, "But, Beth, can you picture living victoriously *today?*"

Yes, I could.

And that's how we did it.

Christ taught me to live one day at a time,

depending on Him alone to "give me this day my daily bread." I can remember in the early days of getting through the withdrawal of addictive sin that I'd seek Him in the morning, then live on His sufficiency until noon. Then until dinner. Then until bedtime. Then the worst time of all: the black of the long night. Sometimes I'd sleep with my Bible open on my chest. Other times I literally slept with it open on my forehead because I knew that my biggest problem was my broken mind. I begged God to help me make it without turning back.

The tears stream down my cheeks as I tell you that one day turned into two. Two days turned into seven. Weeks turned to months. Months turned to one year. Then two. Then three. Then four. Then ten.

I am a woman with a human nature heavily given to sin, but I have not lived out of that powerful old nature in a long time. We are making it, God and I, one day at a time. How I pray I will never again look at life from the bottom of a pit, but all I know for sure is this: "Thus far has the LORD helped me." With the writer of the familiar hymn, I, too, can sing:

Here I raise mine Ebenezer;
Hither by Thy help I'm come;

And I hope, by Thy good pleasure,
Safely to arrive at home.
Jesus sought me when a stranger,
Wandering from the fold of God;
He, to rescue me from danger,
Interposed His precious blood.

O to grace how great a debtor
Daily I'm constrained to be!
Let Thy grace, Lord like a fetter,
Bind my wandering heart to Thee.
Prone to wander, Lord, I feel it,
Prone to leave the God I love;
Here's my heart, O take and seal it,
Seal it for Thy courts above.[13]

We end this book with an invitation to a new beginning. Today is a day of fresh commitment. Go back to that time line and look at the last bold dot on the line that represents your "now." You have already dated it with the present month and year. In an available space around it, add the additional label of "Ebenezer Stone." I want you to picture picking up a stone from the ground presently beneath your feet, raising it high, and proclaiming, "Thus far has the LORD helped me." And He'll help you again tomorrow, the next day, and the next.

If you tumble into unbelief, cry out to God, reach around you for another Ebenezer stone, stand back to your feet, and start walking again. Never forget that long-term victory happens one day at a time.

Lastly, I want you to add a very fitting label to the "..." on the end of your time line. Let me explain: Hebrews 11 is commonly called the hall of faith. It is God's testimony of flesh-and-blood faithfulness. If you'll glance at it, you'll see that the segments follow an inspired pattern:

By faith . . . Abel . . . (Heb. 11:4)
By faith . . . Enoch . . . (Heb. 11:5)
By faith . . . Noah . . . (Heb. 11:7)
By faith . . . Abraham . . . (Heb. 11:8)
By faith . . . Isaac . . . (Heb. 11:20)
By faith . . . Jacob . . . (Heb. 11:21)
By faith . . . Joseph . . . (Heb. 11:22)
By faith . . . Moses . . . (Heb. 11:23)
By faith . . . Rahab . . . (Heb. 11:31)

Gideon, Barak, Samson, Jephthah, David, Samuel, and the prophets as well as countless others implied in Hebrews 11 all lived their lives by faith, gaining the evidences of many promises (Heb. 11:33), yet none received every promise in their earthly lifetime. The explanation? "God had planned something better for us so that only together with us would they be made perfect."

Hebrews 11:40 fittingly concludes the chapter with a reference to us: to all believers who would follow in the footsteps of faith.

Dear One, you are the continuance of Hebrews 11. It concludes with verse 40, but I think God might have each of us see ourselves as Hebrews 11:41. Picture one more verse on the end of the Hebrews hall of faith that says,

"By faith (your name) . . ."

I want to be in that hall of faith. I think you've made it to the end of this book because you do too. We want to believe God for every promise intended for the soil of earth and persevere faithfully until the full inheritance of heaven. As we conclude, if we're serious about making a commitment to a life of faith, let's sign on the dotted line. Go back to your time line and write the reference "Hebrews 11:41" over the concluding ". . .". If you don't mind writing in your Bible, you might also go to the very end of Hebrews 11 and in the small space between the concluding verse and the beginning of Hebrews 12, write what has already been implied:

"By faith (your name) . . ."

See yourself on that page. Picture your vital place in God's lineage of faith. God is not keeping your score, but He is writing your testimony, just as He is writing mine. When He pens the final dot on our earthly time lines, His lasting testimony of each of our lives will be what we did . . . by faith.

Do it, Dear One. Live by faith! I promise to do the same.

If I don't see you here, I'll meet you there. Until then, no more business as usual. From here to eternity, we're *present-active-participle* believing God. Stay a verb. Live out loud. And wake a few nouns.

Never stop believing God.

Endnotes

1. *Strong's Greek Dictionary of New Testament*, #4102, 58.
2. "Old Testament Lexical Aids," *Hebrew-Greek Study Bible*, 1544.
3. Walter Hooper, ed., *C. S. Lewis: Readings for Meditation and Reflection* (San Francisco: Harper San Francisco, 1996), xiv.
4. "Old Testament Lexical Aids," *Key Study Bible*, #2047, 1511.
5. Beth Moore, *Praying God's Word* (Nashville: Broadman & Holman, 2000), 34–35.
6. "Old Testament Lexical Aids," *Key Study Bible*, #4162, 1524.
7. "Memory," *World Book Encyclopedia*, vol. 13 (2001), 392.
8. "Old Testament Lexical Aids," *Key Study Bible*, #1670, 1509.
9. Ibid., #3075, 1518.
10. Quoted in Philip Yancey, *Soul Survivor* (New York: Doubleday, 2003).
11. Rich Mullins, "Creed." Quoted by James Bryan Smith in *Rich Mullins:*

An Arrow Pointed to Heaven (Nashville: Broadman & Holman, 2002).

12. James Bryan Smith, *Rich Mullins: An Arrow Pointed to Heaven* (Nashville: Broadman & Holman, 2002), 43.

13. Robert Robinson, "Come, Thou Fount of Every Blessing."

About the Author

Beth Moore is a writer and teacher of best-selling books and Bible studies whose public speaking engagements carry her all over the United States. A dedicated wife and mother of two, Moore lives in Houston, Texas, where she leads Living Proof Ministries and teaches an adult Sunday school class.